What others are sayin

"Thea M. Kellogg is herself the guide that brings the darkness of depression into light. Kellogg's courage and determination permeate her journal notes and offer insights into ways of finding love in one's self in the radiance of significant others, while facing and coping with the terrors of betrayal, fear, and anger."
– *Clark Moustakas, Ph.D., Center for Humanistic Studies.*

"Thea's book talks about the reality of depression, and how one person was helped to heal herself. If you or a loved one has this terrible disease, get professional help. It is readily available. The chance of success is high. Thea's story is inspirational."
– *Phil Schaff*

"You've touched many tender spots in your story. I saw myself and my emotions a lot in your gift of putting your pen to paper. You didn't spend time looking for gifted words, you wrote from your heart and pain." – *D. L.*

"I just finished reading *Visions of Sunsets*. I am overwhelmed! I felt your pain – and cried; I experienced your anger – and cried; I rejoiced in your healing – and cried. This book must be published! It's compelling and powerful." – *D.*

"Thanks for sharing your life in your book and your willingness to use those life-experiences to help others. I believe the only way of effectively understanding another's feelings is to have lived what he or she has lived." – *E. M.*

"Thanks so much for sharing *Visions of Sunsets*. I read it last night. Your honesty, determination, and courage come shining through – I admire your strength. Your openness and insights will open the door for many others. You're a remarkable lady!" – *S.R.*

"I wish people understood the connection between depression and anger; that they are two sides of the same coin. To say "Why do I feel so bad?" is to kick yourself, to say "What am I angry about?" is empowering. I couldn't believe it – we seemed to be having the same dreams! Then I realized it wasn't that the details were the same, but the language was – a mythical language of symbols that we speak within ourselves as we try to unravel a problem." – *Laurie C.*

"Your book shows your strength and determination to control and combat your depression periods – before, now and those possibly yet to come. This should be an inspiration to others." – M.R.W.

"I appreciate your compassionate honesty and helpful ways; how you've written this book! It's unique and I like the Dream, Thought, Memory, Letter, etc. sequencing. I like that! Yes! God has sparked a flame within you to help others." – V.W.

"Thank you for sharing your thoughts with me. Just finished reading – WOW! How beautiful a journal is as it surely helped you put your emotions (good and God) on paper. It also will help others in being aware of situations in their own life." – E.M.

"Your journal flows so that we can see the healing taking place. You are at the point where you can identify what's going on. If you can identify your depression – always deal with it." – M.

"I really enjoyed reading your book! I can see a lot of myself in this book, as I have had the same feelings and have felt the same way about life before. Because you have opened up and shared all of this with whomever reads your book, you are helping us (at least me) begin to open ourselves up as well." – Juli

Visions
of
Sunsets

My sun has set on depression,
    It looms no longer there.
Visions of sunsets for others,
    My only hope and prayer.

Thea M. Kellogg

Second Edition, Revised

WynnHart Press
Suttons Bay

Many of the designations used by manufacturers and sellers to distinguish their products are claimed as trademarks. Where those designations appear in this book and WynnHart Press was aware of a trademark claim, the designations have been printed in initial capital letters.

With the exception of Dr. Barbara Quinn, Thea's psychologist, real names of doctors have been changed to protect their privacy.

Published by WynnHart Press

Copyright © 1994, 1996 by Thea M. Kellogg
First Printing 1994
Second Printing 1996, revised

Printed in the United States of America

Kellogg, Thea M.
Visions of Sunsets

Library of Congress Catalog Card No. 95-090025

ISBN 0-9645035-3-0

Book and cover design by:
  Cheryl C. Cigan
  Known Publishing
  P.O. Box 251
  Suttons Bay, MI 49682

Inquiries and other requests should be addressed to:
  WynnHart Press
  2481 Setterbo Rd.
  Suttons Bay, MI 49682

To place orders contact Known Publishing at 1-800-450-8618.

With deepest appreciation to:

My husband Ray and children, Curt, Jon and Mark
   – their love and understanding has never wavered.

Other family members, especially Mother
   – without their support this book would never have
   been printed.

Dr. Barbara Quinn, Ed.D.
   – for her caring and professional manner, I will be
   eternally grateful.

Naida and Sharon
   – two special blessings in my life.

Friends, both old and new
   – I find them everywhere thanks to a loving God.

PROLOGUE

by Dr. Barbara Quinn, Ed.D.

Following is a journey through different stations of life experiences in the process of psychotherapy for the treatment of depression. Depression can go unrecognized for many years or perhaps an entire lifetime, but feelings of missing out, being angry but not knowing why, or feeling that something is missing in your life can be descriptors for undiagnosed depression. Others around us, as well as ourselves, may punish ourselves because we *should* be able to snap out of it; whatever *it* is.

Depression can be very painful and may express itself in many different ways in different people by the variety of symptoms or problems that are manifested. Likewise, the treatment of depression can be most effectively dealt with by implementing a multifaceted approach. The focus of treatment needs to include the *physical, psychological* and *spiritual* aspects of a person's being. All are intricately tied together and no single component can be adjusted without impacting the others. After all, we are striving to achieve and/or maintain a delicate balance in our lives which includes all three areas.

During the psychotherapeutic process, journaling is often used as a tool for exploration, memory/recall of various life experiences (perceptions of), and making connections. Integrating this recall of insight regarding those life experiences is possible as we are further removed from the actual experiences by time. These glimpses of personal history are not chronological in presentation and only with analysis and synthesis do they begin to fall into place. As these insights occur, answers to some of our questions can result in that *a-ha* experience.

This book is an account of Thea's travels through some of her life experiences, her discoveries, insights and how they have fallen into place for her. They have provided explanations for many of her unanswered questions. In this process Thea has gained renewed energy to live her life and is wanting to share this new-found zest for life with others so that they too can revel in its light. — B.Q.

INTRODUCTION

When I first began to write my journal during therapy, I hid it. I wanted no one to find it and read it. I made sure it was well hidden, because if someone read it they would surely think I was *crazy*. These writings were about dreams, feelings, and thoughts I would have and they made no sense when I wrote them. They did provide a *billboard* for my therapist, but she never *told* me what to do. My visits to her would cause me to dig and try to reason my plight. I read books, I went to seminars on depression and I found *to look at one's self* has been the hardest job I have ever had to do.

At times I would get angry with Barb, my confidant and therapist. She seemed to *know* the answers to my questions, but kept them. She made me do all the work and it was painfully slow. I, of little or no patience, wanted the answers now! She only smiled and would say, "It will come." To my thinking then she could have shortened therapy, but I know she would have done me a grave injustice. I would never be where I am today.

As I look back over the hours I spent with her, I gratefully appreciate her God-given ability, knowledge and caring manner. She patiently taught me to drink from a coffee mug I use that reads, "There is no elevator to success, you have to take the stairs." I thank her from the bottom of my heart!

Today I share my journal with family, friends, and those who feel the need to read it. I do this freely and without reservation and answer their questions. If this journal helps them understand me, that is fine. I really hope it helps them go on their own search for themselves.

Dream *1: a series of thoughts, images or emotions occurring during sleep; 2: a dreamlike vision: daydream, reverie; 3: something notable for its beauty, excellence or enjoyable quality; 4: ideal - dream-like - adj. dreamy - adj.*

I did not know until a little over a year ago that I could actually remember some dreams. Usually they would disappear fleetingly upon my awaking never to be thought of again. Occasionally a dream would be so wonderful, I would try to recapture it and return to a segment and gently try to grasp the mood. This would never work and I would be on to something else.

With the help of Barb Quinn, my therapist, I discovered I could not only remember, but at times had great detail to write upon when waking. These dreams were not always pleasant, as dreams should be, but they would hold subtle meanings and even sometimes seemed bizarre. Why would I dream of these people, some I haven't talked to in years or ever spoken to at all? I would find myself in strange places I had never been.

I would wake in the morning and maybe just remember several words of the dream and these would trigger the thoughts to flow. I was compelled to write these dreams and thoughts and the feeling would persist until I had accomplished what needed to be done. Some days I would write for only half an hour, the longest was from 7:30 a.m. to 2:00 p.m. Some days were sentimental, some were fun, and some caused tears and pain. The writing still went on.

I had been seeing Barb for several months and she would ask if I remembered any dreams. I began to remember slowly at first and some nights there was nothing. Dreams are interspersed in my writing as they occurred and are marked as such.

Dream

The First

It started in the countryside, I know not where. A row of houses joined together, a hillside behind them and still more houses. They were pieced together; old, shabby, and all needed care. It reminded me of stories I had read or seen of mining or lumber towns in their infancy. It was bleak.

I don't know how I got here. I just was and I was alone. I was also small, perhaps six or younger.

There were men talking in small groups or working on projects. I could walk among them and they did not see me. It was as if I was not even there. I could see everything, but they could not see me. I enjoyed this feeling and it was pleasant and peaceful to observe.

All of a sudden as I moved through this town, I heard someone say, "There's a girl!" I looked around to see her and could not find her. As I turned to search, I looked toward the voice to determine where they were looking.

They were looking at me and came toward me as I watched. It was ME they saw, but how could they when no one else had? I looked around to make sure, but everyone except those few coming toward me worked on as if they did not hear or see my predicament.

I looked away and searched for a spot to run to. There was nowhere to go - only streets. I ran! They followed and sometimes I could get ahead by a long ways and then they would catch up. I darted in and out of streets and would try to hide. They always located me. Finally I saw a depot and a train. I wanted to get out of this town, but the train was moving away and I did not think I could catch it. I did and those chasing me stood angrily on the tracks. I felt relief and entered the train car.

There was only a conductor on board — no one else. He smiled and I sat down. My feet did not reach the floor and I could swing them as I looked out the window.

Cars were added to the train, but we never stopped. The train moved on. The conductor rarely spoke only to say, "You can't get off." I would fool him like the others and get away when the train slowed. It never did!

I grew on this train and the train moved faster until outside became a blur. I knew when cars were coupled up as there was a jolt. The train was long from the original car and I could never get off.

I woke!

Dream

I was with someone watching out a small window. There was an asphalt road winding past our hiding spot, stretching across fields and hills into the distance. Across the street was a cottage with leaded glass windows. The windows were diamond shape, only a few were clear glass.

As we watched, a car stopped and two boys and a girl got out. The girl was drinking from a bottle wrapped in a paper bag. The boys tried to take the bottle away. A policeman stopped. The girl paid no attention to anyone and disappeared down a street.

The boys crawled under a porch. At that time I was across the street in the other house trying to see them. They were talking and looking for the girl.

I was back across the street. As I looked down, the boys had changed. One was a dog of medium size with wire-like hair and he disappeared. The other became a black cat with a beautiful shining coat. I went outside and the cat was friendly. I was not afraid of it and I played with it. It curled around my legs and purred. I sat down on a small bank of grass and petted it. The cat became more aggressive and persistent to be stroked and held. It was not mean. It slowly crawled higher on my body until it became heavy and I leaned back on the grass. Then my legs felt like lead weights were holding them down and I could not move them. The cat moved onto my chest until I could barely breathe. It became heavier still at which time I awoke. Still I felt the heaviness of the cat.

Dream

There were two carloads of people. Some were classmates of mine as teenagers and a couple were my son's friends. We found an old house and decided to go through it. We had to climb over bleachers (sort of) to get in and I could not do it. My legs were weak and I could not lift them up. A neighbor watched us from his car and his grandson was with us. The grandson was sick and I wrapped a scarf around his head and he went on ahead.

I found a door and entered the house to find it filled with antiques and old furniture. The house sat on a high bluff and we could see all over the countryside in the distance.

As we looked over the contents we decided we would each take one item. Another two or three cars pulled in the drive. More kids came, but they were rowdy and began taking lots of things.

A man and woman came and told us to leave, but we refused. We put back what we took. Soon a police car came and they rounded everyone up. We apologized to many people, but they were angry and told us we had to raise enough money to buy siding for the house.

A Memory

This picture flashed across my mind as it previously had done, but this time I recorded it. I have had this happen before and would dismiss it. This time after writing, the thought would come back to me and I would think about it and what it meant.

I was very little, perhaps four, and I can see myself by the lilac bushes in front of the farm house. It was summer and I had on a pale dress with flowers, anklets, and brown shoes. The shoes had a strap that buckled on the side. The toe of the shoe had a design made with small holes to form the pattern. Also, I had braids in my hair fastened with rubber bands.

I played with someone and he offered to show me the pigs in the pen. It was a short walk, but I could not go there alone. I had been told that they would bite and I could go only when they were fed. This person placed me on his shoulders and we walked toward the pen. There were many pigs to watch and some large ones.

We proceeded to walk north on what was called the summer road. After about a quarter of a mile there was a driveway which went to the left. We turned here and there was a corn field. Whoever carried me undressed me, folded my clothes and had me lie down on his shirt.

The memory ends here and it always has.

Thoughts

I went to church this morning and visited Aunt Eleanora at the nursing home on my way. She was sleeping. The house has just been redone and it is beautiful. Mary has a special knack to decorating.

My feeling toward Aunt Eleanora is one of great sympathy. To lie here day after day for weeks, months, and now almost a year does not seem fair. She sometimes knows me, but mostly not. She can no longer speak to any of us and communicates by eye contact. Her needs are met daily by Mary and her staff, especially Linda. She is bathed, changed, fed and in their total care. I am sure she hates this as she was a very private and independent lady. She does enjoy the Interlochen radio station and this is her only form of entertainment.

I noticed when she was still living with us that her mind would take her on mini-trips. She would sometimes tell of being in a neighboring town and how it was growing. At times she would tell me to tuck the girls (Nancy and Patty) in and make sure my younger son's friends were kept away. "No hanky-panky!" The *girls* are now in their forties and I'm sure they would smile. The sounds of our home would remind her of times in her past and she would return there.

This morning I wonder why God is putting her through this ordeal. She attended church and served on committees, made quilts for missions, studied her Bible, and led a life as to set an example for others. Does God protect these elderly from pain as she seems to have none? Does their mind entertain them in their last days?

I also wonder if I will be in this position in thirty or forty years or sooner. I hope not. Mother is going to be eighty-seven in October and we notice a very gradual decline and hope she, too, does not have to face long-term care. She has lived next to us twenty-two years out of a twenty-nine year marriage. She is self-sufficient, very opinionated, and somewhat interfering. I have resolved to never live this close to my children.

MAY 4
Thoughts

Raining this morning and my husband, Ray, is going to Canada fishing for ten days. He leaves tomorrow night. Hope they have a good time. This will be the longest we have been apart in almost twenty-nine years. The boys are here, and I'm glad as I don't like being alone.

Went to the city with Naida yesterday. She, too, has a son coming home and is not looking forward to it. We love them, but it's time for them to leave the nest.

See Dixie in her yard and will miss them when they move. She has been a fun neighbor. Also another family leaving this summer. The neighborhood is changing rapidly.

Ray feels we need to sell in a couple of years. House is big at 3,000 square feet and expensive to run, taxes, etc. Have had it appraised, but no information yet. I do not want to move, but for practical reasons I can see we need to downsize.

Letter

Dear Barb,

I owe you an apology for our Wednesday session. I was not totally honest in discussing why I quit drinking three years ago October. It was an embarrassing time for me and I didn't want to discuss it with you. I've thought about it and decided I need to deal with the problem.

There is a deep anger I sometimes feel. I was angry Wednesday. I had dealt with a security company and discovered after doing paperwork for them twice, they could not locate any of it. The day before I spoke to my brother and his wife about inviting Mother this Sunday. This anger showed itself by my being sarcastic to them. I regretted this later. I feel anger, which I can't direct, because I can't remember circumstances. I need to deal with this.

I thank you for what has been accomplished in four months. I have slowed my pace, found new interests, made some future decisions, spoke to Ray on the *incident* I do remember (which answered questions he had for thirty years). I have discovered I don't have to deal with ALL my problems. I have learned to like myself a little more with your understanding and guidance. Thanks!

Going back to November and December, a couple years ago, I do not remember much except something was terribly wrong with me. The thought of just ending it all seemed the real solution. I don't know why I didn't.

In some of our sessions I feel frustrated, as you are *well aware*. I have little or no patience! It seems to take so long, but then it took forty-five years plus to get here. I recall you stating to have sessions not too far apart. Please give me a call when you have an opening.

Thea

Thoughts

Wrote a note to Barb Quinn yesterday and feel better to be open with her. Also thanked my brother for having Mom for dinner Mother's Day.

Great day today - brunch with Kesner family at The Park Place. Mark and I attended church. He enjoyed the day also.

Made the decision to put our dog, Sandy, to sleep. She has miserable days. We got her in May when Mark was five. He is now nineteen. She has been a great dog and we love her. I think of Jack Kevorkian. I don't want another dog.

Thoughts

Went mushrooming and found a good batch. It came to me as I walked in the woods that my parents and family (some of them) were critical of other people. There would be discussions (that didn't leave our house) about the neighbors and friends. There seemed to be family feuds going on. I guess if we hear this all the time we become this way.

I can remember being self-conscious about my actions. We were told to behave as the family had a reputation to uphold. I think going away to school for four years and living downstate helped me break most of this habit. Ray's parents were positive and so is he. We have tried to do this with the boys.

MAY 12

Thoughts

Met with Barb and we walked for half an hour. I liked this. She related my anger and depression were intertwined. There is an inner struggle. Having been raised in a conservative family, I still feel deep down I am supposed to *behave*, but I really need to do something wild once a week as an escape.

I could confront the problem.

When Mother gets on my case, I need to tell her to not boss and leave. She can make a list of what she needs and call my brothers also.

Boys rooms! Shut the door - she's positive they will grow up to be normal adults and live in clean houses. The more I nag the longer it will go on. The same with Jon's bills and tickets.

What *wild* thing should I do?

Children do poorly in school as a rebellious reaction. They raise Cain as adolescents to show their freedom. They also retaliate by embarrassing parents.

Need to walk in morning.

Feel better tonight.

MAY 17

Thoughts

Ray home from fishing. Missed him! Kept busy in yard, new flower garden, etc. He had a good time and I think he should buy into the cabin group in Canada.

June 14

Thoughts

Went to Docs at Schuss Mountain for weekend. My sister and I shopped and the rest played golf. Great time.

June 14
Dream

I had a recurring dream which involved a mental hospital. There were many patients and one very large strong man. He was outside the door and had to be put in a straight jacket and then put to sleep. He laid that way for days and when he came to he was very docile. The care givers trusted him and removed his restraints. He would, when not watched, kill other patients in a very gruesome manner. Pull off their heads, tear them apart, squeeze them, etc.

Some of us tried to hide, but there was nowhere to go. We hid behind coats, we hid outside. He would shake trees to get us down. Finally we were by an ocean or large lake. He got into a boat to chase someone and a long way out the boat sank. We knew he was dead, but not 100%.

It seemed the dream went on for a long time. I would wake and doze off. It would begin in a new spot, but always the large man in the same setting. Sometimes he was nice and almost loveable and then became angry over nothing.

Thoughts

I can feel some of my old habits returning. I'm getting too busy again, but difficult to slow down. All furniture to be refinished for others I have done. Lawn needs to be mowed every three to four days and it takes five hours. Garden and flowers are planted. We have renters this weekend and much house cleaning and restoration to do.

On Friday I had to pick up duck show items, type duck show pages and return all to Pete. Ray wanted to play golf and said I was short with him. We needed copy paper so I could run off information he needed. I thought he should go to Traverse City and get paper as Char and I wanted to shop around here. He thought we could drop off information at the museum in the morning. We are leaving at 7:30 a.m. and no one would be there at that hour. It was a lack of communication. He has people to phone, bids to figure and he plays golf or ignores it. It's like having another Jon (my son) and I resent it.

July 10

Thoughts

This past week I had several down days and began to think of years ago and these feelings. The first was after graduation from high school. We were into partying and I thought of just walking into the lake one night and drowning seemed a real possibility.

There were a few times during college I was down. After a year and a half of teaching I knew something was wrong and went to several doctors. No real advice was given. One summer a niece and nephew came to visit and we toured all the sights in Grand Rapids. We went to fairs, etc. My thoughts at one point were to spare them from problems. But I couldn't hurt them.

My son was born and we built a house and kept busy. Everything was OK for a couple of years and it was back. I do not remember much of this past fall. I only felt that if I was busy things would be OK. In December I ceased to be able to do anything and thought of suicide. Life was not worth living. I was tired and just didn't care.

Lately, by not having all my jobs and worrying about others, to be in control of Mother etc., there is still something wrong.

Ray and I have done more things together. I have been walking, playing golf, showing more interest, etc. But I feel like I'm only going through the motions on some of these things.

Thoughts

It's been three weeks since I've talked to Barb. The time went quickly, but not always well. I had several periods of anger, but was not able to express it. I have hurt feelings and this turns to anger and simmers. I have never expressed openly why I am angry with someone. Sometimes when I look back at a situation it seems ridiculous. I become moody, but don't want a confrontation. Sometimes I don't know why I'm angry for sure.

When I'm busy things seem to go better, but then I usually have four or five things going on and it gets out of control.

I also feel *retirement* is not really something to look forward to. Seeing all the elderly and the problems they have had is not pleasant. Deep down I don't want to move; Ray would like to live at his parent's home.

Thoughts

Much has happened since last entry. We went to North Carolina in October and had a great time. In November I repainted our bedroom and living room. On November 3rd, I had an appointment with Dr. Smith. Once again, talked about side effects of medications. He only added another anti-depressant. I later talked to the pharmacist and learned some of my complaints were possibly due to pills. Blurred vision, loss of hair, dry mouth, eyes, decreased appetite.

I quit taking Premarin and Provera. December 3rd I had an appointment for a second opinion and had Ray go also. This doctor, Dr. Jones, took me off the second anti-depressant and said it was too much. Stay off Premarin and Provera. I had looked up the side effects and they could cause depression.

It is now a month later and I feel better. I still wonder if this is a chemical imbalance or psychological. Dr. Jones said to come back to him if I wanted to go back on hormones. I'm to see a new doctor (Dr. Starr) in general practice rather than a gynecologist. Also if not better perhaps see a new psychiatrist to go over medications.

There have been some hot flashes and lack of sex drive. Sometimes I am cold to the point of shaking, and have symptoms like a hangover and not being coherent. Sometimes I can nap for an hour or two. This is not like me.

Thoughts

Aunt Eleanora

Aunt Eleanora claimed she couldn't cook really well to get the full flavor. She could sew, but she'd say, "It's just not right," or, "I could have done a better job." In my opinion, I don't think she ever thought or said "I can't teach." The natural ability was there and I will remember her as being a great teacher. I don't just mean her teaching days at school, but about life and how to live it.

She was to me a beautiful lady, inside and out. She cared about people. Her friends and her family were important. Until the past few years, Aunt Eleanora kept track of every niece and nephew and many of their children. A large job considering there were nearly thirty of us at one time. She took pride in their accomplishments, suffered their misfortunes, and grieved their untimely deaths. She was always there for family.

Aunt Eleanora took pride in her home and loved company. To stop and just have coffee or visit could be made special because of her gracious nature. She was glad to see each and every one! She *listened,* she offered advice or let you think about *it,* but she never *told* you what to do. Aunt Eleanora also loved a good joke.

Aunt Eleanora did have rules! They were unspoken rules, but common knowledge. She did not push these rules, but with a gentle way, I knew she had them.

1. Don't swear, especially in front of her. She could give you a look over those glasses which was not kindly. I'm sure she and Uncle Friend had great conversations over this rule. I have, ever since seeing the movie *On Golden Pond,* associated Uncle Friend with Henry Fonda.

2. If you can't say something nice about someone - don't say anything. She saw the positive side in most people.

3. Be patient with people. They're all good; it just takes some longer to get the job done.

4. Have a sense of humor and be able to laugh at yourself. I think of the time a few years ago while having lunch at Bonanza, she made herself a dish of ice cream and the machine stuck in the on position. She ended up I'm sure with the largest dish on record. She just laughed and remarked "Pa said we should clean our plates, but I don't think I can."

5. Fully support and love your country. It may have times of being imperfect, but it is still the best country in the world. Vote Republican!

6. Her final rule, I think, and the most important was believe in God! Aunt Eleanora had a strong faith. She practiced her faith, studied her Bible, and supported her church in every way she could. She gently encouraged others to also. Aunt Eleanora had strong convictions about God. She firmly believed "there will be ups and downs, but God will take care of you." The last several years had been down times for Aunt Eleanora, but as I think of her today, she's in very good hands. This was her final lesson plan!

Thoughts

When I got sick I could not function and didn't care! As I look back it was a long time coming.

I was always this busy person. I took on all kinds of projects. Ray and the boys and the house needed caring for. My mother lived next door and depended on us. One by one, I added aunts and uncles to my list. Many of them had no children and I gave them attention and love. The yard and garden needed caring for in summer. Also I took care of bookwork for the business. There was furniture refinishing that I couldn't say no to, when people asked. There was always *something*. With cousins we formed a corporation and bought and sold property, have a house we rent weekly in summer and monthly in winter. I do the same with Aunt Eleanora's home. When things began to slow down or *close in* I would just add another job.

My children would refer to me as the *Tasmanian Devil*. They would suggest that I had taken too many thyroid pills. They saw and didn't get in the way of projects. They were not neglected, hell, they *were* one of the projects and they had damn well better turn out *right*. In spite of me, they did. They are all three loving and caring people and that's all we need with a lot of truth to get along in life.

Two years ago May, I added another project. I would run this country shop with handmade items. This weakened the camel's back as the saying goes. Then one by one my aunts and uncles got sick. A favorite uncle had already left us and I knew the rest were dying. This was something I couldn't fix.

By November, I would cry for no reason. Life sucked! I tried to pull it together. I bought a new car and barely remember doing so. The new car didn't help. Christmas came and I don't remember doing the shopping or cooking.

When one of my favorite nieces and namesake phoned to say they were coming to visit, I couldn't handle it and just said "No" to Ray.

My mind just quit! This person who had done *everything* was done. I could not do the simplest of tasks and could care less.

There was lots of help to arrive at my rescue. Ray was there as he's always been. The boys pitched in. My work load was taken over by others or they did their own *work*. Naida was always available and ready to do *things*. Relatives and friends phoned and I felt a genuine concern and understanding.

Having thoughts of suicide can really scare you. By the grace of God I had the courage to phone a doctor and get an appointment to find out what was wrong. I had no clue. I just knew something was wrong with me. A very short office call and Dr. Smith informed me I was suffering from depression. I finally had a name for it and it was treatable. I had earlier encounters with this *monster* and never had a label for it. It was a mental illness and I didn't want it or desire to deal with it unless I had to. Now I had to.

Simple as that the doctor had said, "You're depressed." I could cry over nothing. I woke at 4:00 a.m. and could not go back to sleep. I had no energy, lost interest in everything, could not concentrate or make decisions; weird thoughts would go through my mind. I would try to think of *normal* thoughts to get away from the bizarre ideas. It didn't work! I could picture in my mind an area I had seen in England and it was beautiful. A large field, green and lush, with scattered rocks and hundreds of sheep. The land rose up on all three sides to form a huge valley. There was a stone fence and unusual gate at the entrance which looked open. Upon closer examination it had a grate across with holes so we could walk on it, but if the sheep would try to cross they would fall as the holes were too large for their feet. The sheep could pass through another area and instinct seemed to warn them of the grate. I, at 4:00 a.m., would try to count those sheep to change my thought pattern, thinking I would fall asleep. By 6:30 a.m. when Ray's alarm went off, I gave up and got dressed.

Besides the medication Desyrel, which the doctor had prescribed, he suggested I should go to counseling. He gave me the name of a clinic, but I elected to find my own. I wasn't going where crazy people went. After contacting several psychologists in private practice I kept returning to one name. I don't know why, but SHE was the one, Barbara Quinn.

On January 13th, my calendar said "Quinn – 6:30 p.m." This woman, unknown to me, was my choice after several days of agony. I actually was going to a shrink! God!

Notes and thoughts about my first day of therapy:

I really don't want to go to this stranger. I am a private person. There are thoughts I have that I would tell no one. These are my feelings and I wouldn't want anyone to think they were strange or I was unusual. I have protected myself for fifty-two years and now I have to part with my secrets?

The weather in northern Michigan is cold in January and it gets dark early. Maybe it will storm and be too nasty to go out. What does one wear to see this person? Every decision is thought over several times and rationalized. If I dress nice and have my hair done I will appear more *normal*. Maybe I will only have to go a couple of times.

I decide on slacks, sweater, make-up and the whole bit! I'm nervous, apprehensive, and uncomfortable. Ray has decided to drive me in and wait for me. I know he's thinking "she won't go." The twenty mile drive is quiet. Idle chit chat. My hands sweat as they usually do if I don't like something (on airplanes I need a towel) and I could use a restroom.

Entering the outer office it appears small and basic. A table, magazines, six or eight chairs in wood and upholstery, coffee pot, a print of Charlevoix Harbor catches my eye. I like it. The subdued color tones and lighting give a warm effect. Ray and I sit apart and I really don't want to be here.

I don't even know how old this psychologist is, probably in her fifties, tall, thin, motherly, no maybe she's heavy. Probably sits in an office all day. What if I don't like her? I actually feel sweat running down my back in January in Michigan!

"Hello, I'm Barb Quinn! Come on in." She says this like I'm on *The Price Is Right*. I glance at Ray for support and he smiles. The Desyrel that I've been on for several weeks moves me trance-like to the doorway she indicates. Her arm and hand point graciously to enter.

I over dressed. She's wearing casual slacks and a sweater. She is not what I expected! Her age is much younger, perhaps late thirties or early forties? Does she know what she's doing? She moves gracefully, almost cat-like with her long dark hair loosely flowing. She appears small as she sits at a large oak desk and her actions tell me she has done this many times. She's relaxed and I choose a small sofa to sit on. I'm across the room and it's darker here. The mini-blinds are pulled, but street lights show through and it's snowing slightly.

Does she know I'm uneasy? Almost afraid to be here? Not afraid of her, but of her profession and what she will find. Mental illness causes reactions from people that are not kind. There are many jokes and behavior is unpredictable. Will people I know avoid me as I may have them? How does one deal with a *crazy* person? These thoughts come to me as I sit here.

My family discussed people with mental problems and I never felt they were sympathetic. I was told to stay away from several of them. This disease was *unacceptable* and now I had some form of it. I don't know what this woman will find, but I'm not happy to be here.

Dr. Quinn slowly began by asking a few questions. She carried the conversation and I said very little. My answers were guarded. I could play this game. The hour ended and would next week at 4:15 p.m. be OK? She didn't ask if I was coming back. It was assumed I would be there.

The week was long and confusing. My sleep patterns and normal thoughts were interrupted by sad morose times that seemed not to stop. Even with Desyrel, the heavy tired feeling would not leave.

The second visit was still uncomfortable. Family members had an assignment. They had to list all Mom's *good points*. I wasn't sure I had any left and I didn't think Ray and the boys would have time to complete a list. They all three presented me with filled sheets and many of the *points* were the same; loving, caring, funny, smart, great cook, etc. Others included creative, protective, willing to help others, sensitive, good listener, forgiving, and Ray's ended "my best friend." I read their lists and thought these don't describe me. They used to, but not anymore. What had happened? I cried, I worried, and when things got really bad I walked.

The walking amazed those who knew me. I had never exercised! I was a person who would move a car three blocks to save steps. The walking helped as Barb Quinn said it would. I noticed things I had been oblivious to, a change of scenery, and after many weeks the gradual change of season. Spring was welcome, the sun was beautiful and my walks lengthened. Several people would walk with me at times. Sometimes I would take the neighbor's dog for company. Life was bearable.

28

The weekly visits continued for many weeks. Sometimes I felt I didn't make any progress; other times a little. I liked walking with Dr. Quinn on some visits as they seemed more relaxed. She was still doing most of the talking. I listened and could ponder her comments for days and sometimes a little something would *just* fit. I have never been patient and would get angry because I couldn't remember things.

At times I felt all alone and didn't want to talk about the past. I roamed over farm land where I had played as a child, and these walks reminded me of fun times with neighbor kids and friends. Other walks were not as pleasant as my memory would play tricks on me and not release information I searched for. Going to specific spots should jog a memory. Some spots I never reached because I wasn't ready. I was trying too hard and things would not be set free.

After many months of visits I noticed I no longer wrote "Dr. Quinn 4:15 p.m." It had become just Barb and the time. I also noticed a change in my attitude to the visits. I was still guarded, but I looked forward to them. Sometimes it seemed like a chess match. Knowing which piece to move could have such an effect on the whole strategy. Sometimes it just fell into place.

Summer and fall came and went. The inner struggle still was there below the surface. My visits with Barb were stretched out or less frequent. I had to deal with all these thoughts and sort things out myself. Sometimes I felt she *left me out to dry*. It was painful!

In November my doctor had wanted to place me on another anti-depressant. I tried it for a short time. I had many complaints on the Desyrel. Blurred vision, dry mouth, my hair was falling out, still low days, etc. I sought another opinion and was directed to a new doctor by the name of John Starr. He recommended not taking the Desyrel at all, but trying a new one, Zoloft, a cousin of Prozac. What a miracle! We've had to adjust the dosage, but it works. It's been four months and I feel I'm getting well!

I feel doors opening toward many people that have been closed. I've been more open in relationships with them. The anger is gone that I would feel. Probably this is the best I have felt in many years – maybe ever!

Fifteen months ago today I first met this woman I never wanted to know. At this time I feel extremely blest to have found her when I did. I played the game and defended, but she had patience and understanding. There were times when I tested her *abilities* and she let me. Today I conceded, my defenses are gone; I truly need to be totally honest. I no longer look on these visits as a game, my life has become more important. This special person has guided me back from hell and now my thoughts wonder, "How will I ever be able to leave her?" I expressed these thoughts to her on my last visit.

She has a plan!

Thoughts

On Thursday I went to the family farm. I had grown up here and it is now owned by my brother. I had not been here for some time as we did not get along. The farm was founded by my grandparents over one-hundred years ago. They had immigrated from Norway and settled in this beautiful area to raise a family of eleven children. As time went on my father and mother married and came to live with their in-laws and eventually took over farming and the older couple's care until their death. My parents raised five children through the depression and war years and sold the farm to my brother in the mid-sixties. My father died a few years later. Problems developed, as they do in families, and they got nasty, starting with little things and they grew. Some years later, we became estranged and battle lines were drawn. They planted poplar trees on the property line between us. I killed them. We did not wave if we met on the road or speak unless we had to. We were all successful at this for many years. There were many small incidents to fuel this feud as the time went on. A few years ago it neutralized.

My purpose for this visit was to pick up Girl Scout cookies that their granddaughter sold me and had left here. My sister-in-law asked if I had time to sit awhile. Reluctantly I replied, "I guess so." There was small talk about the weather. Spring is having trouble arriving to northwest Michigan after a long extremely brutal and cold winter. She mentions some of her children that I no longer really know or have feelings for. We discuss the election results from the previous day and their outcome. We are sitting in an entry room which doubles as a family room and it's comfortable. Betty tells me about her exercise program at Flex and riding the BATA bus with friends she has made over the years. She has been going quite sometime as she suffered a stroke nine or ten years ago during surgery to replace a heart valve. She moves with a pronounced limp and has problems with her hand and arm. The trip to Flex two or three times a week has become a ritual.

My mind wandered as she spoke. As I drove into the yard I had noticed chinking missing and hanging from cracks in the silo. The doors to the tool shed looked as if they had rotted off at the bottom. They, and the building itself, remained a faded red which had weathered through the years. The doors were not tightly shut and sagged from their weight on the old tracks.

The yard was strewn with tree limbs as if a storm had occurred the night before. But, it's early spring and so bleak. Patches of snow linger and more is on the way in our forecast. *Lake effect* they tell us. This can mean a trace or eight or more inches. We usually get eight. The rose bush, growing on three old wagon wheels welded together to form a triangle, looked as if it had been electrified. The barbed canes stood straight up in bunches as if they were tied. A few stiffly flopped to either side and moved in the wind. The wheels needed paint.

When I drove past the granary, I thought of an old door which was stored there. When remodeling of the house had been done the door was removed and relegated to this safe holding spot. I hoped it was safe, as the granary also looked forlorn. The cement block posts it stood on had been knocked out of alignment by someone or something hitting the building. The door I refer to has glass in the top half. As a child I always thought *Jack Frost* had come one night and painstakingly etched it as he sometimes does. The frosted glass had intricately woven vine and leaf patterns with swirls and com-plicated lines for my small fingers to follow until I could reach no higher. In the summer this door stood open and behind it was a secret hiding place. From what I know not. In winter the door was shut and became part of a hallway complex to the upstairs. If I had a coat on I could hide here and tuck into the corner as the hall was dark and quiet. I could take my cat and she would purr under my coat.

I could see the sunporch outside through the window over the kitchen sink. This porch had been my summer bedroom until I was ten or eleven. The porch had glass windows on three sides and in summer storms I could see the lightening flash and the thunder would rattle the windows. I was never afraid in this room. I would be moved to this room in June and stay until well into September. In colder weather I slept by the north wall of the living room on a small bed with my cat. My brothers and sister had rooms upstairs. I thought of a weather house (German type) that hung on the wall of the porch. It had been my grandmothers. On nice days the small woman in a light dress would be out. On bad days the man in dark pants and blue shirt would emerge. There was a small fence in front of them and a bird on a perch near the roof line. I wondered where it went. In the winter my mother used this porch for storage. One thing she stored there was a cereal which my father would bring home in a gunny sack-like bag. It was huge and we would take a bowl and dip into the bag to get what we wanted. The cereal was sort of like Sugar Crisp, but not as sweet. When we first got the bag and until it was two-thirds gone it was great. Then condensation did a cruel trick. The remaining one-third we took out with an ice pick or knife. It would sit in a bowl in one hard mass until the milk softened it to be edible.

As Betty and I talked, I was sitting in a wooden rocker that my brother uses. Sort of a mission oak in its design and comfortable. My father had one almost like it except for the square wood inserts in the arm rest. The longer I sat here the greater the feeling of sadness I felt. There was an empty feeling like something left me and I couldn't get it back. The feeling was deep and it literally left me. I could feel it go away from me, cross the room, through the kitchen and into the sunporch. Then I felt nothing! I had no feelings for these people, my feelings for the house, the farm, or anything connected to it were gone.

I left bewildered.

Later I tried to reason this out. I thought maybe this is getting rid of the animosity and contempt I felt for these relatives, because it was gone. I did sympathize with their illnesses. Was I forgiving them? No, I don't think so. I just feel not connected to anything there.

As I went to bed that night I told Ray about my visit and he was sorry I felt that way. I had always had a strong attachment to the farm.

Thoughts

Shadow

"I have a little shadow that goes in and out with me,
And what can be the use of him is more than I can see."

ROBERT L. STEVENSON

When I was little and before I had heard of the above poem I looked for a presence in my shadow. My shadow was everywhere I went as the poem goes, but I could not catch it as I wanted to. It mimicked me! I wanted so badly to play with it. I would sit very still and try to fool it. If only I could trick it, then it would have to play with me.

Sometimes when playing it would be ahead of me as if to catch my attention. I would grab for it! It grabbed back! I would become angry as it teased me. Why would it not play?

When I got real angry with this being, I would banish it. I hated it! I played under the trees and it was gone. I had won. I felt mean.

Sometimes from the corner of my eye this being would follow me. It really wants to play now and I would encourage it. It too liked to run, jump, and do the things I did. But much to my disappointment it would only copy and do nothing on its own. I begged it to show itself, I bargained and I threatened. Just a hint, a clue, a flicker that it would emerge. Nothing!

My shadow had another friend and it was illusive also. I had discovered it while playing on the front steps. It would never co-operate to show itself to play either. I called for the dog, Teddy, to come to me. It said "Teddy." I called another word and it answered. I kept doing this, but it would only repeat the last word I called.

I cautiously approached the lower yard where the barn, corn crib, and tool shed stood. They were very large buildings for me to go near.

Where would this person be? I called and no one answered. I called again. Nothing, but birds, chickens, and everyday noises. I ran to the porch and called again. It answered! I had to find the source and so began my exploring of buildings that had not been in my realm.

I searched diligently and would sometimes return to the porch to listen which direction the voice came from. A new plan would develop and somedays I had help. My shadow was there! I made friends with it on search days and *we* looked together. *We* were not afraid to enter buildings and discovered other things of interest. *Our* natural curiosity expanded my little farm world to the boundaries of 120 acres and beyond.

We never found the echo we knew was there and on rare times of visits to the farm I check to see if it's still there. It answers!

My Shadow

I have a little shadow that goes in and out with me,
And what can be the use of him is more than I can see,
He is very, very like me from the heels up to the head;
And I see him jump before me, when I jump into my bed.

The funniest thing about him is the way he likes to grow —
Not at all like proper children, which is always very slow;
For he sometimes shoots up taller like an India-rubber ball.
And he sometimes gets so little that there's none of him at all.

He hasn't got a notion of how children ought to play,
And can only make a fool of me in every sort of way.
He stays so close beside me, he's a coward you can see;
I'd think shame to stick to nursie as that shadow sticks to me!

One morning, very early, before the sun was up,
I rose and found the shining dew on every buttercup;
But my lazy little shadow, like an arrant sleepy-head,
Had stayed at home behind me and was fast asleep in bed.

Robert Louis Stevenson
from: A Child's Garden of Verses

Thoughts

School

When I was little I was lonely. I played alone, but had imaginary friends at my beck and call. My mother refers to this childhood in this manner. "You were so lucky to have such a good imagination you never seemed lonely." She had no clue!

When I had never played with another three-foot person until kindergarten, I had no clue! I remember being put on a large yellow school bus with my brother who was six years older. I carried a rug which was to be used for naps (I never took one). I noticed no one large had a rug. I was different. Short with a rug! I have always felt different.

My brother delivered me to a basement room in the old stone school. The room was freshly painted, the odor remained. The color was cream and it was everywhere. There were wooden chairs in a circle and our size. A raised sand box on legs stood in the center of the room. Nothing in it but sand. I thought how strange! On one side of the room stood a low, long table with chairs on either side. On one end was a shelf unit with paper, pencils, crayons, etc. A large desk was across one corner and here was Mrs. Miller.

Mrs. Miller was *old* (fifty?) and she moved slowly. Today I would call her a grandmotherly type. To me then she was just *old*. I had never known grandparents as they were all gone by my time of arrival or shortly thereafter.

I immediately noticed all (twelve) of these other people my size. Some of them seemed to know each other and began to play. Some of *us* watched them and they ignored us. Eventually we made friends, but all through grade school there was still a difference. *They* were usually the town kids and we were farm kids. If I forgot this there would be remarks from my mother to remind me. "Those town people think they are so important." In my mind they became important and we were not.

The girls played separately from the boys and had games like jacks, jump rope, tag, or hop scotch. I hated most the games, and would only watch because I didn't want to make any mistakes. I discovered books and devoured whole series: *The Bobsey Twins, Carolyn Keene, Nancy Drew, Classics*, etc.

I saw classmates only in school and that was my total contact for many years. The family as a unit did not socialize except for church. There were no clubs or groups to join at the time. We just floated along.

In seventh grade we, from Union School, were joined with students from Bingham and St. Michael's Catholic School. We entered a new building and met new people we would be with for the next six years. Our friendships crossed boundaries of where we lived and went to church. We integrated! I had always thought Catholics were sort of mysterious, especially of interest were nuns. I formed a friendship with Bernadette and learned Catholics were not as bad as I had *heard*. She also had a cute brother, Don.

Joy Arai arrived at Suttons Bay to teach English. This teacher was the first genuine caring teacher we had experienced. From the first day we ALL knew she was different and we wanted to do well in her classes. She challenged us and made learning an adventure that we looked forward to. At class reunions she is always mentioned and all of us smile with our own special thoughts. We loved her then and still do.

At this time I discovered this sense of humor and quick wit I possessed. I used it and pushed it to the *max* many times. I grew rebellious of *correct* behavior. A period of *almost anything goes* developed. We did daring things from entering school at off times, borrowing tests (never Arai's), took teachers' answer books (she couldn't function), played games, drank in classrooms and bowled in the hallways. We were delinquents and it went on for years.

There were house parties, beach parties, boat parties, field parties, and any other type we could think of. We partied on the courthouse lawn and dared to be caught. We drank in cars and rode the railroad tracks. We could go from Northport to Traverse City and get on and off anywhere in between. I drove over trestles that I wouldn't dare walk over today.

Pam and I worked at the drug store. At eighteen I could sell liquor and I would sell to Pam. (It seemed OK at the time. Sorry Claude.) We had decided we should try a variety to see what we really would like to drink. We started in the left hand corner of the pint bottles and worked our way through every shelf of which there were many. The scotch was nasty, but at eighteen we had started this test and we were persistent. We shared with friends, but not always. The irony today is that scotch would be my favorite.

This life style continued in college and everyone thought (I felt) that I was having a good time. I was miserable.

Thoughts

The magic of Zoloft began December 13. I had been on another anti-depressant, Desyrel, for almost a year. It had helped some, but the side-effects were counter productive. There were problems with my vision, dry mouth, a cloudy memory at times, and life would be confusing. I couldn't remember details. I suspected other medications (Premarin and Provera) were causing all my problems. This sadness and agitation stayed with me until after New Year's.

By January I found myself becoming more active. I walked, skied several times and began to read voraciously. My vision was back to normal. I read two or three books a week. I couldn't read enough and I loved it. The best seller list was accomplished and I moved on. I branched off to new topics and found my appetite had changed. I loved John Grisham, Robin Cook, Robert Waller and threw in Danielle Steele for occasional light reading. I even liked James Patersons' *Along Came A Spider*. These books caused a mental challenge and I couldn't leave them alone.

At this same time, I found myself becoming more outgoing. This was a source of amusement to my family. My two grown children would actually sit and have lengthy conversations with me. "Where has this mother been?" I'm sure they thought. I no longer *ragged* on them to do this or that, I didn't keep track of their bills or payments, I didn't care if they did their laundry. Their rooms could rot off the house if their doors were shut. It became their lives and no longer my job or obligation to *protect* them. They loved it! They smiled a lot!

My attention was diverted to a totally new field. I don't know what caused this, but probably a combination of things; my weekly sessions with Barb, *finally discussing my childhood with Ray,* or from taking the Desyrel for eleven months? The past months had slowly opened the door to desired sexual pleasure. But now after being on this miracle drug, Zoloft, after several weeks, it blew the door off its hinges. It began with a look or remark which any dictionary would define as *"flirt"* (a person who plays at love). It grew weekly and reached a level of unbelief. This deep affection and desire which I *always* had under *total control* turned to lust. Pure and simple! I lost self control. My thoughts said, "Hell, let it happen. This is OK, you're married to this man, you fool! You can do anything the two of you want to do." This led to daytime thoughts and plots on my part. Ray for his part, was amused, responsive, sometimes wary, and jokingly remarked, "Twenty years ago this could have killed me had you been this way!" I'm sure he also thought, "Where has this wife been?"

This sense of well-being and mini-high affected other areas. I could converse with people I had always known, but not been comfortable enough to talk to. I saw things in a new way and understood their feelings and reasons for their actions. To actually *listen* to people and not have my mind wander brought their feelings much closer. I could concentrate for longer periods of time and my memory improved. This euphoria rose to the point that I could tackle anything. Oh, I knew what I was doing and I knew right from wrong. It was like I was separate and was fascinated by this new person I had become. I had never in my life felt this way or even thought it possible. Any inhibitions that I had were gone. I liked this new me!

On February 7th, I met with Barb. I had no problems. Life was great. There was nothing I could think of to discuss with her. I'm out of here! Hey it's been fun, thanks! We left four days later to begin three weeks of vacation. Our first night out we got caught in a heavy ice storm in Kentucky. There was no way we could leave the motel the next day. Oh well!

Vacation went well. We visited Fort Morgan, dog races, shopped, walked the beach and saw beautiful sunsets. My favorite was going to New Orleans to Mardi Gras. I had a vague idea of what we were in store to see and experience. We were staying a half a block off

Bourbon Street at the Prince Conti. The bars on the auto entrance and guard at the door I noticed immediately. We soon toured the area and watched parades, drank cheap beer, and began to join others in the bead collection process. Ray was not impressed with the gays, lesbians, transvestites, odors of beer and urine with horse manure mixed in. None of us were prepared for the filth and lack of morality. I was absolutely fascinated with everything. It made me glad I missed the event while in college. I made strong associations with the Biblical cities of Sodom and Gomorrah. They threw beads and condoms; there were couples having sex and exposing breasts, but we didn't even turn our heads after awhile. Young men would freely expose their genitals to balcony holders and be tossed "beautiful" bead necklaces. It was wrong to be here in this mess, but it intrigued me. By the final day, *Fat Tuesday*, the novelty had worn off and we searched out other areas of the French Quarter. Someday we would like to go back just for the jazz festival.

My feelings of well being persisted. There were occasional days of downs, but nothing unusual. We stayed with Chuck and Charlotte at the condo in Gulf Shores they had rented for the month. The area is beautiful and we appreciated their gesture in inviting us. There was some tension between the two of them and we were ready to leave for home. Just the two of us sort of exploring on the way home was nice. We even stayed in Kalamazoo on our final day to delay going home to snow and cold weather. The motel was *nice* also.

While at Gulf Shores, I watched a talk show on which the author of *Listening to Prozac* was being interviewed. He had a guest and former user of Prozac declare how dangerous this drug was. (The man had been over dosed.) I had mixed feelings about taking Zoloft from the start. To take a pill that changes your feelings is pretty scary. Our first Monday at home Oprah had a program on Prozac also. Her show was a much more positive one and they interviewed quite a few users of the drug. By the time I went to bed, I was in tears. These two shows and my own reservations caused me great concern. Did I know what I was taking? At the same time I did not want to have to give up this pill that was letting me enjoy and experience life at its very best. My feelings were one of sadness, confusion, and despair.

I NEEDED Barb Quinn! The next afternoon I was in her office. No longer the flippant and *I'll only let you get so close* person she had seen a month ago. My *magic* had left me and I was petrified. At fifty-two I had become childlike in my reasoning. I was angry, sad, confused and unsure of anything. I wanted straight, direct answers and in black and white and NOW. It had taken fourteen months of many visits, but at that moment I *trusted* this woman. She calmed me and we discussed my fears rationally. I feel an attachment to this woman, I like her. Some days she does most of the talking. It doesn't seem that I've revealed a lot of information. She gets bits and pieces and stores them, she watches my actions (I feel this). "This drug is not habit forming. You are not dependent on it. The shows you watched upset you, but this medication is safe." I asked if she would take it, or if she would have her daughter take it. "If either of us needed it, yes, because it helps!" I left feeling better.

The following Saturday I went to a seminar at Faith Reformed Church on depression. Dr. Meg Meeker was the speaker. She explained, "Depression is anger that has gone under. It's a smoke screen for bitterness. A depressed woman is a woman grieving for a loss." That word anger keeps surfacing. It has taken a long time to emerge to where I can see it and really know it's there. This anger has to do with Mother in part. "She only has as much power as I allow her to have." I have begun to do this. Yes, she still angers me at times, but I now know why I'm angry and it happened throughout my childhood, adolescence, and beyond. There was a feeling I had to do what she said (obedience) and to do it her way.

It's been a lot of little things through the years: Telling us our outside lights were on. "Shouldn't the grass be cut?" "Boys, put your hats on." "Are the boys warm enough?" "If you're not too busy could you 'whatever'?" "What day are you (we) going to shop?" She would tour the house, rearrange the flowers I had put in vases (at times I would jam them in and wait for her to do her thing). She would walk to the garden while I was planting. "Did you have tomatoes or potatoes there last year? Remember to rotate crops. Oh, while I did my garden I put fertilizer on yours, so don't do it for three weeks. Should you plant those flowers there? They seem too tall to be in front." She gets and sorts and delivers the mail. She is on our telephone with an extension. On occasion she listens to my or the boys' conversations. (She claims she doesn't do this.) She has, when I've been gone, cleaned and done my sons' laundry. They get angry! I tell her not to do this. It's their mess, they can clean it up.

How does one live with a clear conscience when at times I hate my mother? We've been taught "Honor your mother and father for all the days of their lives, that their days may be long on this earth." Sometimes I think a shorter life span isn't so bad. Did God plan that if the parent lived to be really OLD the child of this parent got extra doses of tolerance?

Barb did make me actually think about her in a more conscious way. I didn't want to do this before. I remember just growing up. We were provided with all the basic necessities. My mother regularly instilled that we had to behave because my father held public office. The family name was to be protected and we must do nothing to dishonor it. We would have been considered a *conservative* family. This family did not openly show affection. We were not *touchy* or outwardly shown to reveal our emotions. We were taught that "Norwegians are best and we should be thankful we were 100%." Our heritage was something to be proud of and this remains so to this day. One of my nephews, a 50% Norwegian, and a fifth-generation descendent of original settlers proudly displays a Norwegian license plate on the front of his truck.

I remember my mother always being busy. She had a clean house, but sometimes clutter or disorder would occur. This happened usually when she would sew, which she did a great deal of the time. She did, and still does, a beautiful job and her artistry shows in her work. I hated to arrive home from school and find the house in disarray. She did not contain the mess to one area, but it began in

45

the kitchen and sort of flowed to wherever she felt like working. She would be deeply involved in her projects which sometimes went on seemingly for weeks. I do not sew! At this time I realize I hated the mess when I saw it because it meant I couldn't get her attention. She was also busy with chickens, turkeys, gardening, and in summer cooking and doing laundry for hordes of relatives that thought a visit to the farm was vital for their lives. There were of course threshing crews to feed in August, preceded by migrant workers and all their problems in July. Many a time she would accompany a frightened Mexican mother and child to the local doctor. As I write this it becomes clear to me that this woman was almost a slave to her duties. She didn't have time to hold me and read to me or pay a great deal of attention. I don't think she knew how to express love or show affection. Her parents didn't do this with her when she was small.

My mother was number twelve in a family of fourteen. At an early age she was shipped off to live with her sister and be *help* for this older sibling and her husband. At one time she lived with another sister in Lake Leelanau and tells of walking to the farm. At periods she would be back at the farm, but her stays were brief. She has told us these stories over the years with great resentment, but never expresses hate of her parents. It's more of a *woe is me* attitude and how awful her life was. I agree, but can do nothing about it and tire of the repetition of her complaint.

At times I felt my mother was afraid of my father. She would not have thought to confront him about anything. She was passive. She would ask me to intercede to get him to do things. "Ask Daddy to take us for a ride," or such a small thing as "See if he'll stop for ice cream." Sometimes he would be moody and not speak to her. I could sense these times and be very good! He drank and I would run across whiskey bottles hidden in farm buildings. As a child I explored all of these buildings and there were many secret places to hide in, and my imagination conjured up numerous friends to play with. Sometimes I was very lonely.

Thoughts

My feelings of sadness from March 6th persist. My eyes are tired
and dry. I have things to do, but I can't. The weather is overcast and
gloomy. The snow remains at the end of March. I debate whether
to call Dr. Starr and tell him of my feelings. Maybe I would just leave
things as they are. I'm not as high as I was and a touch of melancholy
remains. I'm used to this. They say Zoloft just takes the edge off. It
doesn't change you and it just makes you a little more happy. I did
feel a change! I became less inhibited, more outgoing and friendly.
I knew what I was doing, but sort of like I couldn't control myself.
But yet I did. At times I thought who have I become or, is this the
real me? Sometimes I liked this new me and my carefree attitude. I
do what I want and don't do things to please other people. I was more
aware of surroundings and felt some emotions for the very first time.

MARCH 21

Dream

There is a small girl in this dream and I'm helping her. Sometimes she's out of the midst of things and is on the edge. I can usually see her. Sometimes I have her by the hand and I am guiding her.

She is by me and I see a play cup and saucer sitting on a ledge. The cup has laundry soap in it and is half full. I pick up the cup and wash it out. It's not a matched set, but I feel she doesn't know this.

I'm in a store carrying a pie, etc. I am trying to rent video tapes. The store is in the city and a long way from home just to return a tape the next day. A man I barely know from my village waits on me and he is busy. The girl is wandering around waiting for me. I shop some more.

There are other people waiting for me and I try to hurry. They don't pay attention to the girl. Sometimes I protect her and sometimes I am the girl.

Thoughts

The Book

I woke! My arms are tightly wrapped around my body. My right hand is over my left shoulder and my left hand holding my side and back. My legs are entwined and pulled up. I awake in this position often. I know without looking it is 4:00 a.m. Did I hold myself so tightly I woke myself?

Yesterday I noticed my speech pattern had changed. The sentences were short and chopped, sometimes the inflection was in the wrong place. It was like the new speech pattern college students are using across the country. Annoying as hell to me. Why would I do this? I could hear myself doing this.

I'm afraid! I change position. I may as well get up so as not to toss and turn and wake Ray. My feelings I had after the farm visit remain the same. Or should I say lack of feeling. The sensation of euphoria and that I could do almost anything is gone. The tears are back. The Zoloft has lost some of its magic. Maybe in a way it's a good thing. The ride I was on felt carefree, lighthearted and easy. "Be careful" something said, "don't go too far."

This new lack of feeling for some things causes me concern. How far do I want to travel back to my childhood? Do I think I can make the trip? I don't know what I'll find, but I keep coming back to the thought "you must remember." "Just write it down" Barb said, "and put it away. Something - a word, an odor, a phrase or sound will help someday to remember. Just leave it alone."

I picture a book stack as in a library and there are rows of them. This row is mine. As I move down the aisle, books slide out with titles exposed and then return. "Go ahead and pull me out and read me." "You'll like what you find." These books slide easily — in and out. Some have titles I don't like, but they stick out. Not quite as far or glide as easily; *Basements are Dark*; *The Attic*; *Bed-wetting*; *Room Checks*; *Bowel Problems*; *Knives in Doors*; *Uneasy Feelings*; etc. I've read parts of them.

Some books have no titles and they show just enough to be noticed. They fit snugly in place. I think I could pull them out, but I'm afraid. What's in them? These are the books that intrigue and my curiosity is piqued. "Curiosity killed the cat."

If I write and share my thoughts with Barb or Ray, I feel better and more information slowly flows. My imagination suspects the most awful thoughts. I don't like these thoughts. I, in growing up, did not like to be touched or hugged. After the age of seven or eight - no one did! I would pull away and didn't feel comfortable with their intent. I could hug my children and their hugs back did not hurt me. Sometimes Ray would attempt to hold me and I would stiffen at his touch. I'm sure the first time we made love a cadaver would have been more responsive and warm.

We dated, loved each other's company, and still do. We went on weekend trips either alone together or with friends while in college. We were never intimate sexually even though we slept together. This man has patience with me, and I love him deeply for this.

This past Sunday night we watched a movie together. *Ultimate Betrayal* was about four sisters that sued their elderly father for child abuse. They were beaten and sexually abused throughout their childhood and adolescence. Their two brothers deny this happened, even though the sisters remembered the boys' beatings. They were from a respected and *nice* family. Ray, in watching this movie, saw some of me in these women. The unexplained anger, the need to control my surroundings and people I cared for. My writing at weird times of the night and my obsession to do it. My body language and at times total withdrawal was like theirs. Sometimes my treatment of friends, just to test them, showed. At times I went too far and did damage I couldn't control.

My thoughts as I watched this movie caused me to wonder, "What have I done to my children that I love dearly?" They were never beaten or sexually abused as in the movie. My unexplained anger must have frightened them at times. I myself was never beaten or struck that I can remember. This I am sure of.

Going back to my bookshelves, an area remains. The books on *Sexual Abuse* or *Incest* sit there like a giant time bomb. How do I carefully handle this volume or volumes? Do I pull it out quickly with all my strength and rip it open? I don't think so. I need to hold it awhile and get the feel of it. This book is heavy and I need help. I need help to just get it off the shelf and lay it down. I would walk around it and study it. Maybe nudge it by myself to see what it could do? This book may be alive and snap in anger at me! The feeling that it could also be dead crosses my mind. I like that idea! Then I could slowly open it and at least check the table of contents. If I saw something familiar listed could I read it by myself? Could I then close the book and never have to give a review? Could it remain my secret and only tell part - then close the book? Or is this a tell all book? If it's dead it can't harm me anymore.

But, what if it's not? I *do* know this morning the book is not blank!

Thoughts

Session with Barb

I gave Barb my notes which were pages of two week's dreams and thoughts. "Does everyone bring you written sheets to read?" I asked. "No, just a few through the years, but yours are different." I interpreted that others may have had lists or brief notes and I handed her typed sheets just as I had the thoughts or dreams. Again I had a question, "Is this why you wanted me to keep a journal?" Barb said, "If you write thoughts and dreams down you can get *them* out. They can be referred to and reflected on. They are *out* and you can put them on a shelf."

She held the pages and asked if I could give her a synopsis. There were many and we only had an hour. I replied, "No, you have to read all of it - it's all there." She read and we discussed as she went along.

As to Mother, I don't hate her. I only hate some of her actions and the ways she manipulated me and others. She had a tough time and doesn't know how to deal with problems anymore than I did. What is her role - does she know?

We discussed the girl in the dream. I'm protecting her and always have. As a child I gave her imaginary playmates, and there were two or three. They did what I wanted them to. We had tea parties and made mud pies. We all four would dress my cat and Fluffy also played this game until she would disappear. I could talk to these friends and reply for them. They were always there when I wanted them to be.

MARCH 24

Thoughts

I liked yesterday's session with Barb. I took a sleeping pill at 11:00 p.m. and slept until 5:30 a.m. Ray said we had a storm in the night. Thunder and lightening! "I missed it." "Not entirely" he said, "your foot moved over and touched me at the storm's height."

My day would have been one of duty a short time ago. Mother needed to go to do some shopping and we *needed* to visit her eighty-four year old sister. I had been home almost a month and had not visited this aunt. She had phoned several times and I had called her. She insinuated I was mad at her for something (Guilt Trip). I had laughed and let it slide. I was not angry with her, I had been busy and in truth I just have been doing what I *wanted* to do. Today I was ready to deal with the two of them. They are four years apart in age, but have characteristics and mannerisms to identify them as sisters. For a stranger to meet them together they can be sweet, charming, funny and wonderful grandmotherly portrayals. They can tell stories of their growing up in a family of fourteen. They were at the tail end of this family in birth and today they are the last of this generation.

My cousin one time described his mother as "bossy, interfering, Norwegian (stubborn), and at times a genuine pain in the neck." After all, she *is* my mother's sister.

They can both be fun, but some days the old sibling rivalry will surface and they will not get along. It amazes me that after all these years when now they only have each other left that they can't get along in harmony. Two hours is usually enough!

My cousin (her son) is unique! He's changed jobs more often than the states he's lived in, which were many. He does have a special gift that he inherited from his father. He's a storyteller! I think he drinks to excess like I did, but he's a likeable person. The stories of mining gold in Mexico and escaping with it or becoming an entrepreneur in Traverse City and selling *menuda* (??) from a vendor's cart are fascinating. He has bits of gold he shows and photos of events he tells about. We all know he is embellishing parts of these stories, but his wife speaks and interjects her addition just enough to lend these stories credibility. We wonder as the stories grow with our diminishing liquor supply where will this end? Or if the ending will be different from the last telling.

My aunt has always been someone I loved. As I grew up she and her family lived in California and Mexico. They would return to northern Michigan for infrequent visits. To me these visits were filled with laughter and let the good times roll. She was an "Auntie Mame" type character and then she would disappear for several years. No letters, phone calls, sometimes just a Christmas card. My mother thought her irresponsible and unthoughtful. I thought she was neat! I looked forward to her visits.

My sister lived with this aunt for awhile when they both were working in Traverse City. On one occasion when Charlotte arrived home after work she heard the washing machine running. It had been running all day, unattended, and the clothes were in shreds from the agitation. Aunt was blitzed! My sister shares my mother's opinions. I love this story as I love the aunt. I could have done something exactly like this.

I'm sure my aunt had the same type childhood as my mother did, but she stayed on the farm. She endured the battles my grandparents and their new daughter-in-law and son waged. Her life style was a generation ahead of me, but she and I are alike. I truly discovered her nature twenty years ago when she moved back to the area. I have enjoyed her company.

Dream

There is a house in my neighborhood and it has large stones in front of it. They are huge boulders and we have to crawl over them to reach the house. An elderly neighbor is eating bread and doughnuts with another neighbor. I can see them through the door, but they won't let me in. There is a storm and it becomes raging; there are other kids outside. They let none of us in.

MARCH 25

Dream

A cooking contest is going on.

Ray, my husband, is in part one of this contest. He is eating Corn Flakes. He eats, crosses the room, gets more, returns, eats, etc. He wins in this contest.

In the next section two girls are using special pans to cook or bake cakes. These are pineapple upside down cakes. In one cake they forgot to put in the pineapple. I cut it in half and serve it. Kids eat it, and it is the winner.

The third has me with special pans and cookbooks. I'm cooking with someone and then alone.

At the end the two girls win over all. We feel they did not do this fairly. There was no pineapple in the winner. It was a mistake.

This dream is hazy and drifts.

Thoughts

When I told Ray, my husband, last summer about my memory of last April 20th, I felt as though a curtain had lifted between us and we have grown much closer. This memory has been hard to deal with and it keeps surfacing. I try to put it away, but it will not stay put! We have discussed my feelings and this memory. It will come to me in greater detail someday.

Thoughts

Curt

I spoke to Curt on Saturday. I was sorry I woke him as I knew he had had a long week. The plane crash at Pope A.F.B. had occurred on the previous Tuesday and he was there. He said, "Two days seemed like two weeks."

"Mom, it happened so fast, they didn't have a chance." I could hear the sadness in his voice. He's 6 foot, 3 inches tall, 200 pounds, seems 3 feet wide at the shoulders and I just wanted to hold him.

He described the mid-air collision, the fireball, crash and chaos following. He spoke of helping move wounded soldiers and all the help that flowed in. At times there was too much help and they had to be held back. He told how he took younger guys to the side and talked to them so they could finish *clean-up*.

Curt is in special investigations with the Air Force. This past week his work *sucked*. He photographed every body and helped in *bag and tag*. His manner changed and he became cynical like characters did in the old M*A*S*H* series. They used bizarre humor to forget their feelings. "Didn't need fast speed film." Tears came to my eyes.

The boys or young men killed or injured could have been the same soldiers we saw in October. Or they could have been anyone's son, husband, brother or father in training. We saw them standing on the edge of the tarmac in full gear with parachutes. They would move in lines to the open plane, load, be transported, get in position and jump. They all looked too young to be doing this.

On a warm October afternoon, Ray and I drove to the Sicily Drop Site to watch maneuvers. There were campsites, tanks, trucks with mounted guns, jeeps, and the large drop area to the east. These men could have been anywhere in the world it seemed until the sandwich wagon drove up to sell them chips, gum, etc. We silently watched them and as they went about their duties. I remarked, "Some of them look like they should be home having milk and cookies." This thought came to me as Curt spoke.

"Hey, the President showed up. We had two hour's notice and I was in the van next to his car. Should have seen the Secret Service men check us out. They did a great job on such short notice. My crew took a photo of me with Air Force One. I'll send you one."

"Did Shelli tell you when she phoned that our neighbor JD was killed?" "I could see JD's trailer, as Curt spoke, on its lot with no trees and little grass. The tarmac scene appeared in my mind. We had been given a private tour of the area in October and had been at the spot where wreckage was later strewn. "We did a body search and cleared all but the wreckage; it stays there until investigation is complete. There's a memorial service on Tuesday." All of this sort of rolled out of Curt in a monotone. I could tell he had insulated his feelings.

"Curt, we love you and how are you handling this? Are there counselors to talk to? This is pretty heavy." His reply told me things I had not heard. "This is the fourth time I've had to deal with bodies and I've known some of them. Remember the girl in England I had to track down that hung herself in a wardrobe? I knew and worked with her. I get my mind set so that it's just a piece of meat by the time I get there."

"My God," I thought, "how can he do this and think these thoughts!" He continued, "I feel bad, but somebody has to do it. Besides, their souls or spirits are gone - like JD when I found him. It wasn't JD anymore - he was gone." A revelation hit me, "Curt, I'm glad to hear you say that. All that time in Sunday school, church, and confirmation you *were* listening. While I thought you enjoyed looking at stained glass windows you really were thinking!" He laughed, "Yea, it's more than a place to hang my hat."

59

We spoke of other things that day. Their plans to start a family. They have been married five years and have had to depend on each other and know they want to be together. They will be good parents; they both care.

"Love you a bunch, and there's an Easter package due to arrive with Kilwin's and Murdick's fudge."

Curt and Shelli will be fine.

Dream

I am on the summer road and helping burn huge piles of ???? Two men are fighting each other about getting it done. They do things to sabotage each other's efforts.

A group of people on the north end began to gather. An old classmate is there and I talk to her. There's agitation going on. She grabs me to help me. She changes and I don't understand. She becomes aggressive to me and I am small.

She holds this bag up and it has golf balls in it. It forms to a huge phallus and is laid upon me. I'm frightened, but more bewildered as to why she is doing this to me.

March 27

Dream

I'm on a hill by a large country club. There's an ambulance garage with Greyhound busses and lots of confusion. I am on the roof of a Greyhound and the driver is going too fast. We pass another bus. I'm a little scared, but "Leave the driving to us" pops into my mind so I should be OK. The road is cement, steep, and curvy. It's dangerous, but I don't know where I'm going.

Thoughts

5:30 a.m. The shower is running. Jon has to be to work at 7:00 a.m. He likes his job he says. I lie here sort of feeling in a semi-awake state.

I think of Jon. He was the happiest of babies. Always good natured and liked to be held and read to. I will never forget the story of *The Pokey Puppy* as it was one of Jon's favorites. He had blond curly hair and big blue eyes that smiled quickly. Those eyes still smile, but the hair has darkened and receded. Jon was never demanding, he has Ray's patience. He is tall, good looking, charming, and at twenty-four has no idea where he's going or how to get there. Not a clue! It scares me! He needs a keeper. We all think this and Ray and I verbalize it to each other.

Jon is a dreamer. He has always had his own little world. It was neither here nor there, but sort of spacey. Jon will look into my eyes as we converse and pretend he's paying attention. He looks attentive, but I know his mind is on something else. It wanders.

I love my memories of this little boy and I love the traits and personality he possesses. He has a soft heart for people and cares about them. He does for others and likes their attention. I see myself in Jon.

A sense of humor has always been needed in our family. We have tried to teach them to not take things too seriously - laugh, but learn from mistakes. As a young hunter Jon got lost in the woods one fall for hours. He was always kidded when he was going hunting or on a new venture to take his *orange ball of string*. Later, as a sales representative, he flew throughout the U.S. or drove from every direction out of Chicago. He drove in Germany and England on business. He always found his way back. He can do it!

He cannot or will not handle his personal affairs. He quit his job in Chicago and returned home two years ago this September. He worked in the city six to eight months and took classes at Northwestern Michigan College. He hated the job and switched to a restaurant last spring. This past fall he started at a home for troubled girls and will work part-time at the restaurant this season.

Jon cannot manage his time or money. He has had an auto repossessed, credit cards over charged and shut off, he didn't pay income taxes and owes the State of Illinois $1,000.00 + and the I.R.S. nearly $11,000. (We have an attorney and an offer of compromise is expected which Ray and I will pay to get rid of them. He would never catch up at 24% interest.) He forgets auto insurance premiums until they lapse and seems to have no worry if he drives without insurance.

He goes to the gym, plays golf, eats out and generally blows his money. He doesn't know where it goes. He doesn't pay us his car payment or offer to pay any rent. He owes parking tickets from October.

As I write this I feel sad. Did my control of *everything* also control Jon to the point that he didn't have to be responsible?

Jon has testing coming up in April for any type of learning disability. If this shows a problem, we need to do something to make him independent.

MARCH 31

Thoughts

I called Dr. Starr after a waiting period to see if there would be improvement (there was none). He changed my prescription to 75 mg. from 50 mg. of the Zoloft. It should take a week or two to see if this works. Some negative thoughts persist and a reclusive feeling wants me to withdraw and stay where I am. I'm hesitant in following through on a training program with the Literacy Council. It's a volunteer position to teach reading to adults. I'm not sure I can even do this.

Thoughts

The *magic* is back, but I do not have the mini-high feeling of euphoria, there is just a normal way of handling events.

My attitude has changed or should I reword that? My real thoughts, ideas and feelings are openly expressed. I've gained a confidence that I thought was gone or I never had. I like this Thea that has surfaced. She does what she wants to do regardless of others or their opinions. But not dangerously so or harmful of others. She can come first and consciously thinks of this.

Not all my feelings have changed. I still love all of the people and things I did, but maybe deeper and with more caring. Even to listen to classical music for longer periods of time and enjoy it to a greater degree is noticeable. Before I could only half listen and in short spurts, my mind would wander. Before I could not concentrate and was easily distracted. I now can sit for longer periods of time and read and reflect.

Ray and I have enjoyed our 7:30 a.m. coffee time and have had conversations involving everything. We have known each other for thirty-two years and this week discovered we had been living with strangers. There are no secrets and we learned of each other's frailties, share hopes for our children, concerns for each other, and discussed our future. (Yes, Barb, even Northport.)

Mother has her own phone! It's amazing how this simple move has helped. I've also not backed down on her manipulating of painting her entry way even if she is having company. It needs to be done when I have time, weather is warmer, and I feel like it. I did a *Bat Day* (a term of endearment) on Friday and actually enjoyed all three of them.

I sent in my application to the Literacy Council about teaching adults to read. I'm not sure I want to do this, but will do the training.

They only offer training twice a year and I can decide after. I contacted the Probate Court, but got no response from Leelanau. Grand Traverse sent information.

This past week or two I enjoyed the company of a new friend. Debbie is forty-two and also has depression and it felt good to help her. I wondered if I was doing the right thing? She needs to find a therapist. (Ask Barb.)

This week a friend and neighbor died suddenly. He left his family in shock. I did the usual cooking, visiting and attended the funeral. His wife will need extra emotional support in months to come. As she, alone, will have care of a mentally handicapped daughter aged twenty-four. I also think of my favorite nephew. He worked daily with Clyde and will miss him. We worry about a relapse for Ken, but he has a strong A.A. support group. He has found himself also!

Dixie, my neighbor, informed me while she delivered a dish to the family of Clyde, an acquaintance has asked her about me. "How is Thea? I heard she had a *breakdown*." I love Dixie's answer! "Have you seen Thea lately? She looks great! You must realize that she had some stress with all her old people and three or four of them died in the past year. But she's alive and doing lots of things so I guess she's OK." At first this bothered me, I wondered what people did think? I saw *the acquaintance* at the funeral and hugged her and asked about her family and remarked I had not seen her in months, etc., etc. She looked bewildered and I loved it!

Something concerns me. I do not have the ambition or initiative to do projects that need doing: shelves in my wardrobe, Dodie's three tables need finishing, the yard needs tending, walls need washing and general spring cleaning should be done. Garden could be planted, flower gardens cleaned soon, etc.

I cannot make myself tackle these projects! Why?

APRIL 12

Memory

Have left alone *obsession* of childhood and one day as I was changing clothes a thought came to me. So simple!!! I couldn't figure why I got mixed flashes of a corn field, wheat field   or whatever. It dawned on me there were different times, but I *feel* it's the same person. Some of the books on my bookshelf relate to this. (Barb)

Self-esteem?

Thoughts

Session with Barb

Discussion:
I don't do the above things because I have different priorities. I have done some raking and the other will come.

The *book shelves* probably relate. Leave it alone and in time it will come.

I will not like leaving this woman I have come to depend on. "We will broaden your field and include others like Ray or people you trust. I may not hear from you for awhile or longer and something may come up. I'm only a phone call away."

Thoughts

Referring to my thoughts of March 13th.

Time has passed and I now feel and know this was forgiveness. I can forgive past actions and let it (hatred) go.

I do not have to agree with them or even like their behavior, but I don't have to hate them. Families throughout history have had their differences so we are only one of many.

I was wrong also, perhaps they will forgive me?

Thoughts

When you're little and family members tell you about brownies, fairies, the Easter Bunny and Santa Claus, you trust and believe them. Then you discover it is all false; you're still young and you feel dumb.

Then they tell you about Jesus and God and take you to church and expect you to believe them. I always felt just maybe this wasn't true either. They would attend church and do some things, but not take active parts in services. They were never readers or helped with communion. They may have been council members, but I never can remember them doing so.

Some of the members that attended, my parents did not like. I always thought this was weird to go and talk and be *friendly* and later discuss their bad points. This did not show me trust. They did this with some neighbors also. The family is reserved and does not openly express emotion. They would never have reached out to strangers to invite them to attend church. They would worry about what people would *think* of this religious behavior.

We moved back to the area when our children were little and we started to attend church. I have a strong sense of history here. My grandparents, along with other Scandinavian families, founded this church over one hundred years ago. The family always attended while I grew up. I married here and my children were baptized and confirmed here. My roots are here.

We lapsed in attendance for many years. I returned a little over a year ago and it was strange. I returned alone and sat near the back, always on the left side. I was uncomfortable returning, as I wondered what members were thinking. As I sat here in this pew where my ancestors had probably sat and looked at the same stained glass windows they had, emotions and memories flooded back. Christmas pageants, confirmation classes which bored us at the time, Bible studies I attended, Eda Lafferty as a teacher, waiting for Anna Bahle to slowly move from the organ to the piano to play for the choir, watching two older brothers use the hearing devices during the service, remembering Mrs. Gronseth sing solo in a clear soprano voice. Sometimes we sat in the same pew as Mr. and Mrs. Johnson and my brother and I would get in trouble. Mr. Johnson had Parkinsons and the pew would shake and we would start to laugh. This gained us dirty looks in church from my mother and a reprimand while driving home.

Sentiment ran high those first few Sundays back, but it felt *good* to return. The atmosphere and formal Lutheran Liturgy felt like an *old shoe*. I had missed it and thought about why we had left so long ago. The time we had missed.

We had left in bitterness over a comment made by a member that had *ticked* us off. Of course we didn't approach the member to see if it was true. Why confront someone? It was easier to avoid this person. We would go sometimes and send the boys to confirmation. There would be arguments between members over petty matters, and it just didn't seem worth going. We slowly drifted away and no one, except two families, said they missed us. We had discovered Charles Kuralt on Sunday morning and drank coffee. It was easier.

This was one of my *down* times and I got mad at God! Why should He be any different? I got angry at a lot of people. Usually I didn't even know why I was angry, it was just there.

I have this wrestle with God. I need to keep control, but yet, I know and believe He's everywhere and is all knowing. Why can't I just give in and let Him have the control? It sounds so simple.

Dream

This is a beautiful dream and it starts on a long stretch of beach. In the distance is a huge tower-like hill and it is high. There is a winding road that completely goes around this tower leading to the very top of the hill.

On this long stretch of beach I see a sunset which is magnificent and I walk toward it as if it has a magnet to draw me closer. I reach a closeness and then there is another sunset further up the beach. I am puzzled, but feel the sand and hear the waves and move closer with others joining me on this walk.

This second sunset is every bit as beautiful as the first, and just maybe, a little more intriguing. I look back and the first setting is still there, but up ahead is a third sunset. Others begin to notice and by the time we reach the third setting much further down the beach there are a lot of us.

Something tells us, not a voice but a feeling that there are five sunsets to see in all. If I hurry I will see all five at one time and they will be awesome! We all follow the winding road which leads us up. Some are moving slowly and others at a rapid rate as if it would all vanish.

On the sides of the winding road there are people hugging and kissing one another. As we reach the first sharp corner to turn and proceed up there are couples having sex on the grass and along the banks of the hills. This is OK and we do not stop or even pay them much attention. Here is the fourth sunset and it's serene and tranquil.

We move upward and finally reach the top. The area is flat and has a huge meadow. There are couples everywhere and all engaged in totally beautiful sexual encounters, myself included. There are no feelings except love and what a beautiful area this is. It has been almost a race to get to this summit.

This whole panoramic sight was breathtaking and almost reverent in feeling. There I was. A wholeness and complete love existed here in this simple meadow. All five sunsets are on my left and were now all in a row.

This dream was repeated three times to me in exactly the same way. One right after the other. I have never dreamed it since, but it is etched in my memory as being peaceful and at the same time astonishing!

APRIL 20

Thoughts

As I sit here on a rainy, dreary day my outlook is much brighter. We had sunshine yesterday and it will return tomorrow. We need this rain; "April showers bring May flowers" and mushrooms. "Into every life a little rain must fall." Sometimes I feel like I've been in one hell-of-a flood! But I had a clean-up crew of Barb, Ray, the boys, friends, resource books I *was led to*, and above all God.

I was angry with God for many years and it showed. I was angry with everyone and everything, so why not God? Being raised Lutheran also caused me GREAT guilt at this anger. I didn't know why I was angry - it was just there. Unrighteous anger! I had this tug-of-war going on inside. I needed to be in TOTAL control until one day when I sincerely prayed for God's help. I just gave in and let Him have part of the control. It sounds so simple! The door has opened, cautiously at first to test the water, and the pressure is constant to have it burst wide open. When I lessened my self-will and let go things began to happen. I can't fathom that I have even written this! My total control of everything is no longer my responsibility. The load is lighter!

This morning it dawned on me the benefits of my being depressed.

1. I was forced to take a good deep look at myself and make changes I would never have done without this condition.
2. Most of my anger is gone and the rest shelved because I "don't HAVE to search for it."
3. Made peace with my mother. I know where she's coming from and "she only has as much power as you give her."
4. Closer relationship with Ray. OH, YES!
5. Let my children *go* grow. I had a button once that read "If you love someone, let them go. If they don't return, hunt them down and kill them." Not as funny as I first thought. I need

to get my children to leave the house and I now know they will come back.

6. Express love to my friends and show it freely. I've surprised some of them.

7. Made me read numerous books:
    Care of the Soul by Thomas Moore
    You Are Not Alone by Julia Thorne
    The Road Less Traveled by M.Scott Peck
    Six Pillars of Self-Esteem by N. Branden
    and many more.

8. Some I haven't even thought of.

I have a concern. How can others reach out sooner and seek help from this illness? When I think of the time in my life that I've lost or wasted it angers and saddens me. Times have changed over the years. The stigma of mental illness has lessened. We, as a people, are educated and more awareness is present. Some of us have more compassion because we've been there. We read, see movies, and TV has given us much coverage of going to psychologists or therapists, etc. I know because they find me in my everyday life!

I didn't *know* about depression until I was told I had it. I had no clue - I just thought everyone's life *sucked* (I don't like this word, but it fits) at times. Life sometimes does, but not like depression. It consumes us! We fall and there's little to hang onto on the way down. Sometimes we don't know we're on the way down. We know something is wrong, but cannot express it. Then we hit bottom with all the symptoms: weight loss, we can't sleep, we can't concentrate, we're tired, there is loss of interest, anger and sometimes we are suicidal.

I felt all of these symptoms and I'm recovering. Does everyone have to go all the way to the bottom? I've tried to remember if I could have gotten help, would I have accepted it???

As I stated earlier, *things* have begun to *happen* that are sort of a phenomenon for me. I have been in my own home, shopping, visiting or even taking a class to give my life a new *cause* or *worthwhile purpose* and acquaintances, friends, and total strangers sooner or later tell me they are depressed. These people are usually on a medication (Prozac, Zoloft, Paxil, etc.) but they are talking to NO ONE or using other resources. They're still depressed and don't know why. It's like I'm wearing this neon sign that says *this person will help you. Ask her!* It's weird! I didn't know there were so many of us. Have I become so open with people I relate to them? (Ask Barb.)

Sometimes I just listen to them; I don't comment except to tell them I've gotten help and they should think about it. They don't go right away, but the seed is planted and they usually call and ask for other information. It takes some longer. At times they are so confused they don't know how to do the simplest of things. We've made appointments together and I've driven them to doctors and Community Mental Health. I've mailed them information we've discussed and written them letters about my experience. They get help and are getting better.

They need support to go through the first steps. The comments I hear are, "That's how I feel, you *know*, I'm not alone," or "You wrote this for me, it's what I'm thinking," or they just start to cry and say, "Thank you, I feel better."

APRIL 20

Thoughts

Reflecting on Jon from March 28th.

Jon's testing results show he is fine. He lacks motivation and a sense of direction. We have changed our attitude and control. In the last several weeks he has improved. He has begun to take responsibility even in little things.

APRIL 23

Letter

Naida,

I came to you when I needed someone. I was desperate and had I not stopped that December day, I would not be here today. Having not been to church for so long, I did not feel I could go there. I knew deep down that suicide is against God's law and you are so close to God. You were there!

I actually heard you all those times you were frustrated with me about attending church. It all came through, but I was angry with God. I was angry with everyone, so why should God be any different? There were days when I was angry with you because you reminded me of *things* (church, boys and church, good times we had and at this time I was miserable). Oh, I know I tried your patience! I tried to shut you out of my life some days and I withdrew into my own world and work. If I do enough and keep busy and do *good things* the pain I felt should go away. I didn't even realize what I was doing. You kept knocking on my door – you were there!

Lately, I feel better most days. I've had time to slow down and reflect on many things with the help of Barb Quinn, Ray, family, and special friends. I have come to realize I will probably always need to take a medication for the rest of my life. This is a disease I can more freely discuss with people and in doing so have helped three others obtain help. As I have helped these people, I think of you and what you did for me. You were there!

Something bothers me. The past sixteen months while I've been going to therapy I was totally involved with *Thea*. This is OK, I can come first and I do count. My ideas, thoughts, feelings, hopes and dreams are important and I now express these ideals more freely. As I look about and divert attention from myself to those I love, I once again sense someone special to me seems to be hurting. She has *down* days, some days she's angry, some days she's quiet, and some days she withdraws. Some days she's happy or puts up a good *front*. I recognize that good *front* because I walked in those shoes for most of my life. As this person freely discussed God and let her emotions show, I would like to do the same because she was there for me.

Love,

Thea

79

APRIL 24
Thoughts

Returning to April 15th and my control of God.

The door has opened ever so slightly and the pressure is constant to have it burst open and never close. When we lessen our *self-will* and *let go* things began to happen. I can't fathom that I have written this. My TOTAL control of everything is no longer my responsibility. The load is lighter!

April 25

Thoughts

In referring back to when I titled the book, I have tried to delve deeper.

A month has passed and I have let these thoughts ferment. Did something *really* happen as my memory tells me, or is this pure fabrication and *misguided* thought? Barb's words come to me, "You don't have to remember, you can leave it alone." Her understanding look as she says this — what does she know? Why does she leave me to struggle? I have come to love this person that I didn't want to know sixteen months ago. But she doesn't make it easy. At times, I get angry at her. Then I suddenly realize she can't tell me; there is no easy way. This is my struggle. *I* have to do this and it takes time.

My patience has improved. I do know the anger I felt is lessened and I can't *fix* what happened, but I could forgive those who hurt me. "Forgive us our trespasses as we forgive those who trespass against us."

APRIL 26
Thoughts

In order to be able to go for counseling, we need to be made aware of resources available. We need to be encouraged to actually go and seek the help we need. We also need a gentle push now and then along the way. My family physician checked me over for the complaints I had given him. He ran many tests and finally stated very simply, "You're depressed, I'm giving you a prescription for an anti-depressant and you should seek some help."

It is now nearly seventeen months later and in retrospect I think and verbalize, "Why did it take me so long to actually go and talk with someone?" I realized years ago (thirty-three to be exact) that I needed *someone* to talk to. I even gave it a try!

I was in college at Northwestern Michigan College, confused, angry, and unable to function. This went on for days and weeks. In desperation I located a psychiatrist. I phoned and his rates were high for a college student without steady income. I could not ask my parents as I felt they would think I was *crazy*. I saved enough for one office visit and went to make the appointment. His office was in downtown Traverse City on the second story along with others that did business from this building. What if I met someone I knew? How would I explain why I was here? Would they even ask? I was miserable! I left!

The telephone was easier. It was much safer. I called and explained my feelings and finances to him. I will never forget his reply, "Well, first you're going to have to tell your parents, as I expect to be paid." I looked into the receiver and hung up the phone. Today I would call this man an insensitive, unprofessional (@#*^%) jerk! Then I was lost and totally alone and had no where to turn. I stayed afloat for many years by the *grace of God*. I could not concentrate and with no real direction it's a miracle I graduated from Central Michigan University.

It hit me at graduation! I was a teacher. Why? I would have to actually work at this job. My goal was just to graduate and make my parents happy that I had succeeded. I did it for them - not me! I did teach for several years and hated it. One fall I was to *teach* a room of mentally handicapped eigth graders a section of American History and one of English/Literature. I had never been prepared to teach special education and this formidable task loomed all summer. I resigned in August!

I became physically ill. I had headaches, was tired, did not eat, etc. All three doctors I saw missed depression. I don't know how I recovered. There were times I remember voices coming from the radio and it was off. This really scared me to say the least! I never have wanted to face this again.

At ages thirty-eight to thirty-nine this sadness started again. I would cry for no apparent reason. I had a beautiful new home, three healthy children, a successful husband and I was miserable. I had a great neighbor I would visit and just cry. I couldn't talk to her - I did not trust anyone. She didn't know what to do, but I couldn't be alone. I was suicidal, I drank to excess, but I also had three little boys that needed me and a husband who cared. Again, I don't know how I recovered.

This last time when I doctored and he said "You're depressed," *IT* finally had a label, I wasn't *crazy* and neither is anyone else. I had heard of people being depressed, I could deal with this - maybe. There was a ray of hope. I was fifty-two!

Thoughts

The Shirt

A new white sweatshirt with a cartoon on the front that I *had to have* hangs in my bedroom. I bought it several months ago and have never worn it. It came from McGuirer's Irish Pub in Pensacola, Florida.

The cartoon has a duck dressed in Irish green sitting behind a bar with an empty glass beside him. The caption reads, "I'll have what the gentleman on the floor is having."

As I look at this shirt I am uncomfortable. I can't wear this shirt! Twenty-five bucks shot! Why did I buy this shirt? I stop — I bought this shirt because it was hilarious at the time. I actually waited in line for this shirt. What happened?

It dawns on me! The light bulb goes on! This shirt was going to be part of the *cover*. The Thea that frequented bars, drank to excess, did bizarre things to make people laugh and like her would have loved this shirt.

I regard this object with disdain. What I once would have worn anywhere I can barely tolerate. I put it away! I could think of no one I knew of to give it to. My feeling is no one should want to wear this shirt.

The feeling goes deeper than the fact I'm glad I quit drinking. The shirt represents a way of life I lived for thirty-five years and don't like or want to return to. I never felt comfortable in bars. They were smoke filled, noisy, crude, smelled and the bathrooms were usually the pits.

I did a test. We revisited a couple of old favorite spots. We had dinner at Stubb's with Steve and Debbie. We went to The Happy

Hour for dessert (chocolate cream puff). Then on to Omena. I drank tonic and lime and observed. The old group was at Omena, still playing cards, drinking beer, and the atmosphere had not changed.

We didn't stay long.

APRIL 28

Thoughts

I kept a safe distance from people. I have always maintained it. I've tried to reason why. Like if I get too close, then I would lose this person.

My sister is my closest sibling. Not in age (thirteen years older), but in feeling. She, too, is kept at a distance. I would make sure I did nothing to really anger her or she would disappear from me also. She has a quick temper. I can remember when she worked in Traverse City and would come home after work. I always had the table set. She thought if the table was ready, dinner would be prepared. (My mother taught me this.) Maybe my mother had not even started dinner, but with dishes ready *it* was coming. My mother avoided her anger also. She would do Charlotte's laundry and iron her clothes. My sister could be defensive. She has mellowed, but she still can be an angry person. She will tell me she doesn't like people. She has always bought things for the people she does like. It started with *me* (I think). She would bring me toys from Traverse City when she worked. I was five or six and loved the attention and the gifts. This was weekly if not more often. She had a boyfriend who would come and bring her a box of Whitman candy every week. I got the whole box! It got so he (Fred) would drive in with his father's Cadillac convertible and just hand me the candy. Wonderful man! She came to visit us for a week and I gave her all my writings to read. She was fascinated and read from beginning to end. At times she would remark, "I didn't know you were so lonely." At the end she handed me my book and said, "I'm glad I'm not depressed!" I still think she is angry.

I have other family members whom I feel drank to excess besides myself. This was and is for some a way of life. My brother, Jerry, was first to quit drinking over fourteen years ago. We get along better since we both stopped drinking. When we drank, we were defensive and easily angered.

My brother, Darwin, (ten years older) seemed angry to me in his youth. He was wild, he drank, he drove fast and had numerous accidents. He fought with my father, he quit school, he would leave his work (farm) and go off with friends who happened by. He did daring, attention-getting and dangerous things. Fixed old buggies from the farm and rode them down steep hills with ropes to steer. They were almost killed. When things got really bad he joined the Navy. His anger always showed in his behavior and the rest of us hid it better. Darwin always seemed different. He also gave me attention when I was little. He took me for walks, he did wood-working and made me a table and chairs and my mother and he painted rabbits on them. The chair sides were like the shape of a rabbit and painted as if the rabbit was dressed. One winter he made me a snow house by our farm house. It was big and he formed furniture from snow. He covered it with water and it froze and lasted a long time. He would play with me in this igloo. My brother Jerry never played with us. Jerry and I are friends today. Darwin is estranged from me, I'm not comfortable around him. I don't know him, perhaps I *could* make the effort to communicate. They say it is never too late.

When Darwin left for the Navy, my mother insisted we have a family picture taken. After the picture arrived it was only a short time before I scratched my face off the photo. I hated myself — What could have been so awful? I was only ten or eleven. I cry as I write this. I'm sad! I try to remember when Darwin left. Was he going to come back? Would he die? Did I do something so that my father made him go away. I blamed myself because he left.

I've talked and written about my mother, but not much about my father. When I was little I worshiped him. He was the one who held me, ate my pretend mud pies, had tea parties with me, read me stories, rocked me and I was special.

He's been dead for twenty-six years and I feel nothing. There is sadness when I do think of him. I think of him holding public office, his friends, how intolerant he was of my mother, his whiskey bottles around the farm and his anger. I don't know why he was angry, but

I know he drank to feel better about himself or cover something up. His anger surfaced easily.

As I grew older there became a distance between us. It started when I was maybe six, and just grew. Did I do something? This was the first person I lost by getting too close to. I didn't want to sit on his lap anymore.

From the time I was little until maybe five, he would read to me on Saturday night. We would be alone as my mother and sister and brothers would go to town to shop. He never read to me in the living room or kitchen where his rocker was. We read in bed. I remember the bedroom and two large favorite story books. One had rhymes and the other stories. The green one was for stories, but we always read the red one first as I liked the rhymes. I could remember all the words and would correct him if he would try to skip places.

He had an odor of his own which people do sometimes. His was of skin, hair oil, snuff (he chewed and tobacco smell would linger) and maybe a touch of alcohol. I can remember the scent and almost smell it today. I remember the stories, poems and bedroom totally. I can never remember after the stories. I would awake the next Sunday morning in my bed and it would be all over until the next Saturday.

May 1

Thoughts

This Sunday morning an *unusual* event took place.

Ray and I attended church and sat in *our* pew. Darryl Johnson joined us and sat at the far end. I recall thinking, "I don't ever think we sat in the same pew over the years." He was later joined by his daughter Laura, who sat on the other side of him by the window aisle. As church progressed, Laura moved closer to me. There was room for three people between us at least. She still came closer to me until she leaned on me. I smiled to myself, but made no movement. Her father attempted to coax her back as if she was bothering me. She became insistent and actually pushed against me. I put my arm around her and felt wonderful. This feeling of love flowed between us. I was amazed as I had only spoken to her on one other occasion. I wanted to hold her and asked if she wanted to sit on my lap. She could hardly wait and as I wrapped my arms around her, I loved this little girl I hardly knew.

I was aware of the people around me and that some of them who knew me *well* were amazed. I had always been distant and not really touched by people. They had sensed this over the years. This six year old child had me in the palm of her hand! I could do nothing, but return the love I felt from her. Naida, my closest friend, at the communion rail, stopped assisting and looked as if to say, "What's happening?"

We talked quietly as she sat on my lap. I asked her about school and if she like it. She said, "No, sometimes I get bored." I said, "I bet you like to read?" Her face lit up and she replied, "I'm only in first grade, but I read at fourth-grade level." I could sense the intelligence and then she said, "Sometimes I make mistakes." I quickly replied, "We all make mistakes, but we learn from mistakes and that's OK." She accepted this answer and smiled as if she was in total agreement, but needed to hear it.

We hugged some more and rose to sing the closing hymn. The touch of Laura left me as quickly as it came. This wonderful God-given encounter we shared remains with me. I have never felt toward anyone the love I felt at that moment with this six year old. She made everything OK in my life when I was six and now maybe I helped her. I hope so.

It dawns on me that she may come to me again or never sit on my lap again, but I had needed her that morning. It gave me back the six year old girl I had stopped loving so many years ago. God had moved us together!

May 2

Dream

A dream last night needs to be written.

The dream is *nice* and flows along. There is no conflict in this dream that's bad. There are questions that I don't remember, but they are there.

This little girl that I know (maybe me) has this problem, she tells me about it while a nephew (I don't like) is present. She had been in school and got marked wrong on a problem she tried to solve. She showed me the problem. It was a *learning tool* I had never seen before.

It was like an old *Viewmaster*, but smaller - just the two round eye places you would look in (black plastic). It showed a scene and she had to give the correct answer to what she saw. Was the answer spring or summer?

It was an awareness question and had to deal with deductive reasoning. There were clues, but she had gotten it wrong and didn't know why. "You look," she said. I did.

The scene was from the front of the farm house, but only the steps, flower garden and sloping yard, and an older woman were in the picture. There was grass and the woman had a sweater. The scene moved!

The old woman came towards me. Her arms were outreached. The grass was green, the flowers were tall, it looked like a beautiful summer day, but the woman wore the heavy sweater and looked cold. I looked closer - were the flowers actually bushes? Forsythia or something else? Was the grass a little lighter in green than I thought? Why would she wear a heavy sweater in summer?

No wonder the little girl couldn't figure this out – this was too hard for such a small girl. I had trouble!

91

I gave the tool to my nephew to look at and he said, "Easy, it's summer." He had only glanced into the thing. I got angry, "Look again," I said and explained my position and what I saw. We argued.

From around the corner came a woman. She had the answer capsule. She knew the answer. She wouldn't give it to me. I begged for the little girl's sake, so she would feel better. The woman clued us. The answer could have been either spring or summer, but we had to find out on our own. We were angry and I woke.

MAY 2

Thoughts

My answer came quickly and I was compelled to write.

The cemetery is a place I've always liked to go. It's small and I know many of the names. Old Norwegian names — Mork, Solem, Martinson, Bahle, Everson, Moe, Setterbo, Anderson, Gilness, Johnson, Glommen, Larson, and the names go on.

It's peaceful here — I like it. I read the stones and wonder about the people lying here. What kind of lives they led, where they had been, were they happy?

I reach our lots and know *their* positions. I was taken here many times as a child. On Memorial Day flowers were always planted and there was one red and one white geranium at each grave.

"Don't walk on the Hansons" I would be told as if they could feel my footsteps. I still try not to step on people on my visits. Also I never would run and play here, I felt a respect was due and almost would talk in hushed tones so as not to disturb them.

One family grave I always stop by is my Aunt Ella's who died at the age of twelve in 1907. This always made me sad. I have a charcoal photo of her which always hangs in our house. It was taken just before she died. She had a little sister who also is buried next to her, but this grave doesn't intrigue me. Maybe it's the picture. I visit out of a sense of family duty.

I fertilize, mow grass, water flowers, trim by stones, and would plant an extra flower at my father's grave. Many times this was done after a reminder from my sister.

Lately the geraniums are gone as it's too hot and they die. We instead arrange two urns and place them on either side of the headstone for all of *them*.

This year I will stand at my father's grave with no extra flower. He's been gone twenty-six years and I don't feel this loss. Sometimes I think how he treated my mother. In later life he was better, he drank less and most of his anger was gone. He mellowed also. Did he regret what he did? Maybe? At his funeral I was in shock. I've thought about him through the years and I don't miss him.

I know what Barb means when she says "it will come" and I don't have to remember *everything*, I don't have to go back. It comes back a little at a time and God only allows what I can handle. I can kick his tombstone, wonder why, and not feel guilty anymore. I can forgive him, but I'll never take him flowers anymore . . . .

MAY 10

Thoughts

For the past few weeks and months I have had unusual encounters with people. Too many coincidences. The strangers I've met who just seem to have a problem, etc. I treat these people openly and with understanding because I've been there and they know it. I don't always know how, but vibrations carry this feeling.

For the past few days I've been tired. I'm drained and do not want to think about what I call this new *gift*. I need to learn how to handle *it* and be comfortable.

Thoughts

On a warm May morning, to leave Suttons Bay and drive north on M-22 while listening to "How Great Thou Art" would erase any doubts there is a God. To get beyond houses and condos and reach a panoramic view of the bay takes your breath away. The water is green and turns into dark blue and looks as if it goes forever. A slight haze on the horizon, but clear sky overhead, reaches the water and is endless.

There's a lone fisherman in a boat and not a movement from him, nary a ripple, on this vast smooth expanse.

The trees of various greens are just beginning to resume life after our long cold winter. Daily, leaves slowly open as if watching a time-release film. The birds have awakened us in the early morning for several weeks. We all discuss the first brave robin. The bluebirds are back arguing with sparrows and blackbirds as to who gets the house.

The ducks have returned to the 45th parallel. Soon this section of shoreline will be combed daily by tourists looking for Petoskey Stones. Each thinks he is the first to search here and it's so accessible. The rocks and stones are turned over by hundreds each season with each one hopeful and some are lucky. Natives know where they can be found by the hundreds in a short time. We have them in drawers, boxes, on tables and some in jars with water to show their beauty. Our Petoskey Stone spots are like our mushroom areas. We keep them secret to protect our supply.

We curve along the bay and I notice I drive slower enjoying the feel of M-22 as well as the view. The dips and turns are familiar.

I reach Raftshol's vineyard and Warren is tying up grapevines. There are new plantings of grapes where I remember cherries growing years ago. Warren has cleared more land, it's been hard work. I'm reminded of what it must have been like for early settlers. He didn't just have someone come in and clear in a short time. It evolved slowly and each year he cleared a bit more. I think of him exercising his faithful companion, I smile. He drives past our house slowly in his car and the dog runs alongside and seems to enjoy every mile of the trip. One day Mrs. Raftshol drove past in this same way, so I take it as a family way to exercise the dog.

Belanger Pond is on the left and I *always* turn my head to look. It's beautiful in all seasons. As a child I loved to sit in the backseat, as my children did, and just before hitting the bump the car would accelerate and my stomach would flip flop as we traveled over the bridge. We would expect it, but it was sure a wonderful feeling when *it* happened! The bridge was restructured several years ago and the experience for a new generation is gone, but I can slightly feel the thrill in my memory.

There was a grinding mill here years ago and flour was made from the grain provided by neighboring fields. This flour nourished many large families in the area.

Rock, the hermit, lived near here in an underground home he had dug into the side of a hill. I always wanted to find his spot and I've wondered about this mysterious man and how he found Leelanau County.

Thoughts

Naida and I returned from Florida and both of us had accomplished what we felt we really went for. For my part, Sharon and I cleared the *air* and problem between us. Naida and her siblings have become much closer and it showed.

I have been thinking how to handle this awesome gift of grace. I have wrestled with these feelings and it is uncomfortable a little of the time.

"Many are called, but few are chosen," Matthew 22:14. I have always found this to be a strange statement. Why would only a few be the chosen ones? Why would God pick and choose? Then I read M. Scott Peck's interpretation in *The Road Less Traveled* and think I am most comfortable with it. "All of us are called by and to grace, but few of us choose to listen to the call."

The song "Amazing Grace" takes on a whole new meaning for me.

Some days I ask, "Why me?" Then when some event happens and I feel this grace utilizing me I love it. I have by trial and error discovered I can't force it, capture it, or control it in any form or manner. It comes to me on its own terms and is not MINE to dominate. The only power I have is to push it away and it is getting harder to do so.

There are days when I am tired from *thinking*; questioning why this is happening to me. I am forced to sit, slow down and nap! Spring is a wonderful time of the year to walk, ride or just *be* and observe nature return to life around us.

When I see what He does during this season, I marvel and am reminded how He works in us. We too have seasons, and I feel in the spring of my life at fifty-two.

Amazing Grace

John Newton
(1725-1807)

Amazing grace! How sweet the sound
That saved a wretch like me!
I once was lost, but now am found,
Was blind, but now I see.

'Twas grace that taught my heart to fear,
And grace my fears relieved;
How precious did that grace appear
The hour I first believed!

Through many dangers, toils and snares,
I have already come;
'Tis grace hath brought me safe thus far,
And grace will lead me home.

And when we've been there ten thousand years,
Bright shining as the sun,
We'll have no less days to sing God's praise
Then when we first begun.

MAY 16

Thoughts

Reflecting on the dream of May 2nd involving the girl, and of Laura in church. I saw myself in this child as I held her. I became the six year old I was loving so deeply. I could finally love me.

The dream of May 2nd is complicated. I am the small girl and I have a problem. Laura, in church the day before, mentioned she sometimes made mistakes and in my dream I focused in on my problem (a mistake had been made, but I didn't do it). I, as a little girl and as someone of fifty-two, could solve the question of *Spring* (did something happen to me, and could I put it to rest?) or *Summer* (nothing happened, and quickly get rid of it as the nephew did). Either way I would be OK. I deeply felt this. The woman with the capsule was Barb telling me it was my problem and I had to solve it myself and no one else could give me the answer. The months of digging, thinking, and remembering were almost to come to a close and it was time.

I still wonder about the older woman walking toward me.

Thoughts

Reflection on March 21st, the dream involving the small girl.

The half-full cup and mismatched saucer represent to me partial care. As she is little, she won't really *know* this. She gets some attention, but not the full amount needed. Therefore the half-full cup. The laundry detergent represents work and the reason for lack of attention.

The shopping shows how busy times were and in the confusion there was never a full amount of time. Also as she's little, she won't remember other *things*.

May 27

Thoughts

As I reflected on my notes from April 20th, I have reached a conclusion. I was concerned for others and how they could receive help and not be afraid to deal with their problems.

We can be here to help each other. We need to be aware of people and their problems. We can listen to them and pay attention to their clues.

We cannot push them. They must do their own journey, however long.

I think of myself and my journey so far and am reminded of he third stanza of "Amazing Grace" by John Newton:

> Through many dangers, toils and snares,
> I have already come;
> 'Tis grace hath brought me safe thus far,
> And grace will lead me home.

Thoughts

In re-reading March 17th about the euphoria, I think I may have figured out why I felt this way. When I started taking the Zoloft I still had residual effects of the Desyrel in my system. These chemicals sometimes stay in the body for up to eight weeks. So it was like I was on two anti-depressants until the one was depleted.

Others I have talked to do not experience euphoria when taking Zoloft without previous drug (anti-depressant) history.

Thoughts

On April 18th I had this fantastic dream.

To walk on this beach and feel the beauty and realize that sex is OK and it only gets better until we reach the top is a revelation for me.

The symbolism of seeing all five sunsets in a row and their magnificence impresses on me (three times) that sex is not only to be enjoyable, but an act which God created – like my sunsets, to be enjoyed!

JUNE 6

Thoughts

The previous eighteen months have been ones of an intense investigation of myself. Some of the results were painful, but they needed to be uncovered and exposed. By having these memories revealed to me and to know finally the *answers* I had wondered about or suspected — I am free. "The truth shall set you free." This quote pops into my mind and I know the feeling and its meaning in great depth.

Some have questioned me as to why I am not angry. They feel I should be raging. The fact that two people I had loved had abused me and I have forgiven them is hard for others to understand. I will try to explain my answer.

Well into my therapy a thought came to me, "In order to reach where I'm headed, I have to know where I came from." This thought kept me digging when I could have left it alone. Friends would say "leave it alone," or "it's all in the past, what good will it do?" Recovery doesn't work this way and I *had* to know.

Oh, I had anger which I carried for almost fifty years. On May 2nd I realized this anger had to leave me. There was anger over what I had lost in my childhood . . . *and this was innocence.* My whole life could have taken a different turn in growing up. Perhaps I could have been an open trusting person with no need for being on a misplaced guilt trip. Had I trusted others, I would have had closer relationships. I didn't even trust Ray totally after twenty-nine years of marriage. To be involved with anything sexually had been wrong until I confided to him of my memory. The veil of secrecy was gone and with his help, my trust grew.

With lots of help I have come to understand these *memories* were not my fault. I was just a little girl and did no wrong. They did! They may have thought I was too little to remember what was done and that made it OK. As I grew older they felt they were on dangerous

105

ground and they quit, I feel for this reason. I repressed these happenings as children do when *things* are painful, but the dreams of my unconscious gave me clues little by little, as I could handle it, and it all came back. Barb was right again, "leave it alone and it will come."

This anger was replaced by sadness, a sense of betrayal, and I questioned WHY? Alcohol had been abused in my family, by my father and his father before him. It is still a problem today. Alcohol allows people to do things they would never do without it. I'm sure my father must have anguished over this betrayal as I had adored him. The second reason I come up with is conjecture: It may have been an angry or not so angry adolescent going through puberty - curious and exploring. Perhaps he, as a child, had been abused - I will never know. When I tried to find where they were *coming from* and their reasons, my forgiveness to them came slowly. Most of my anger left me that warm May morning as I sat in the sunshine on my bedroom floor and cried. The rest followed, and I began to grow.

The depression I went through was caused by all of these events and the life style I developed to cover my problems. As Dr. Meg Meeker stated, "Depression is anger that has gone under, it's a smoke screen for bitterness. A depressed woman is grieving for a loss." Until we know what the loss is we can't deal with it.

We as children usually don't verbalize our problems. We use a different approach; we send messages by wetting beds, having bowel problems, checking out bedrooms for intruders, and we use knives in our bedroom doors to keep trespassers out. We withdraw into ourselves because it's safe and we don't want to be touched. My mother and others missed these clues and this is why I have had unrighteous anger directed toward her at times. We have discussed some of the anger in our household while I was growing up and we have reconciled our differences. I now know where *she's coming from*.

The spiritual aspect of my healing has always been present. As I controlled everything in my life, I also controlled God. He or She (if you like — I don't) was regulated to Sunday morning service table grace said by one of the boys, and necessary other functions. On April 24th I lost this control willingly and He is in control. To love others, we must first love ourselves and to assist others, we must first help ourselves. I did this!

"Amazing Grace" has worked marvelous wonders in the past few weeks. It has been an absolute joy to share these thoughts, dreams and pages with others who are struggling with their own problems. We all search and make it so difficult. If we could follow Dr. Meeker's advice it could be so simple; what you can't handle just give it to God. He's up all night anyway! For people that have learned not to trust in anyone but themselves this is difficult. We usually hit hard on the bottom when we fall, but we do pick ourselves up, with God's help, and "there's no elevator to success, you have to take the stairs!"

Letter

To Nephew

Dear Harold,

Nice to talk to you last night! I told you I would follow up with a letter about the railroad fiasco.

Some eight or nine years ago, Grandma gave me a stock certificate for two shares of Leelanau Transit Company. We also have two shares from Ray's father. We like the certificates as both fathers were represented and we intended to frame them.

We were approached twice to sell them, once for $50.00 and once for $100.00 a share, we refused to sell. On March 16th of this year, I received a letter from Jonathan Roth stating they could be redeemed for $1,800.00 a share. Ray and I discussed this and called Jon Roth. He agreed to return the canceled certificates to us if we would turn them in. On April 12th I sent a letter and the certificates to him.

As you may or may not know, Grandma loves to play the contests through the mail. She gets "Readers Digest," "Publishers Clearinghouse," "Michigan Bulb," and numerous others. She has never won which is usually the case. She hopes to win big and be generous to everyone.

Ray and I decided to surprise her and even though she gave me the certificate, I feel I took it for sentimental reasons and the money actually belongs to her. She is to be eighty-eight in October and survives on Social Security of about $500.00 a month. She uses the interest from a $5,000.00 C.D. to pay toward her fuel. For the past several years she couldn't make it and Aunt Charlotte and I gave her money to meet her needs and extras.

I was surprised when she told me your mom and dad asked her where the certificate was. She asked me if I still had it. I told her it was already sent in for redemption for her. I don't know what to tell you at this point. When the certificate arrives I feel it does belong to you. She gave it to you first! You also wanted it for sentimental reasons as it has your name on it. I will see that you receive it. As to the money, I feel that is Grandma's decision. For her to do something for you in the future would be easier for her.

I especially feel bad that this incident has to involve you. Grandma and I love you very much. There are only a few of her grandchildren that give her attention and you have always been one of those few. You always take the time to stop and she appreciates this effort.

We have talked and I know how you feel about other things and I don't want this to cause you bitterness or anger. You already carry around too much anger – I know! I don't want in any form or manner to add to it. I don't want you to feel gypped or cheated again.

During the past eighteen months I have been going through a serious depression. With the help of medication and extensive therapy, I'm recovering and feeling wonderful. There was a great deal of information I learned during this time. I would like to share several points with you, not accuse you of these things, but to be aware of hereditary problems.

We come from a family that does not communicate very well, if at all, at times. We protect our *real* feelings and we should learn to deal with them instead. Ask Kenny about this sometime. When we don't express those *real* feelings we carry them inside of us and they are usually angry feelings that we don't want to handle. When I was angry (at friends, your folks, Grandma, everyone else including God) I just took a drink and the problems went away. I could complain to others instead of confronting the issue. I quit drinking sometime ago and with God's help I hope this remains.

Grandma and I have, after fifty years, begun to communicate and I have learned we come from a family of alcoholism as well as a tendency toward depression. The two can go hand in hand. My grandfather, Otto, was in his early life an alcoholic, Grandma feels. As I look back on my father's (Harold) behavior I would classify him as having problems in both areas. He hid whiskey bottles in farm buildings, he drank to excess, he could be moody and not talk to my mother for days, and he would become angry over nothing. He was not always pleasant and we worked around him. Alcoholism is a disease as your brothers will tell you. It starts with a drink now and then and works its way into our life style and we don't notice until sometimes it's too late. It descends from generation to generation until one generation realizes and has the courage to seek help and say, "enough, my life and family are too important." Your generation has begun this and changed the pattern.

I'm not accusing you of being an alcoholic any more than I think you're depressed. I want family members to be aware of both of these problems as they exist. "Depression is anger that goes under, it's a smoke screen for bitterness. A depressed person is grieving for a loss." When we carry years of anger around and add to it, eventually we can become depressed.

I have learned a new technique in my eighteen months of therapy and many $$$$ later at $80.00/hr. I love you so it's free. When someone makes me angry, I tell them carefully, honestly, and leave out my ANGRY feeling when talking. I explain my problem and get rid of it, then I don't carry it around and add to it daily, weekly, and yearly. I needed to go to the source of my anger, deal with it no matter how painful, and forgive those who angered me. THIS WORKS!

Have you ever told your parents why you are so angry? We always think people know why we are angry at them — sometimes they have NO CLUE. They don't know about all the years that your brother angered you. They don't know your feelings until YOU tell them. Write them a letter and, even in that anger I sometimes see in you, remember they deeply love you. They, too, have problems in communication, but open the door and you will be amazed.

I love and care about you and that is why you have received the longest letter I think I have ever written. God Bless!

Love,

Aunt Thea

P.S. Always give God your problems at night! He's up all night anyway!

JUNE 11

Thoughts

It's Saturday 6:15 a.m. and I wake early expecting rain. It has not arrived yet. I have no plans for my day ahead. This is unusual and I realize how much I have slowed down.

I see Barb on Monday — what will we talk about? How was her trip? Did she enjoy the mode of travel by motorcycle with her husband? She did this out of love and a sense of adventure, I feel. Her patients, if they knew, were apprehensive about her welfare. We kept them in our thoughts and prayers. I found her a key chain with a logo for a Harley Cycle. If it was turned sideways it became a cross. The clerk at Classic Cycle had never noticed this and was surprised. He remarked, "Hey, I'm Catholic so I know what you mean - this is perfect." He seemed happy that I drew this to his attention. I don't think Barb took the key chain with her - it was the thought I wanted to convey. They would be safe!

Since seeing Barb last I have thought much, talked to new and old friends, done a great deal of writing, and questioned where do I go from here?

In sharing my time, and listening to all of these friends and then sharing my own experience with them, it has helped them, and me, to grow. They know they are not alone and their problems all vary in content.

One day at lunch with a new friend she explained problems in her life and that she had been depressed, sought therapy, found God, etc. I suddenly thought, "Why am I here?" I had told her about myself, my journal, and how I had shared it with others. She read only the section I wrote about my visits to Barb which I carry in my purse. Her reply hit me! "Maybe we are meeting today because I'm here to tell you that you need a vehicle for your writing." She smiled.

I considered her ability with a computer (she owns her own word processing company) and then I smile at her as she radiates a sense of grace. As others have found me lately - I have found her! Yes! There is a God and He works mysteriously!

Her remarks made me look at my writing — is it OK? Does it hang together and make total sense to others in *all* areas? What do I have to do to learn this? I immediately think of my high school English teacher and I telephone her. I explained that I have been writing and I would like her to read it. She sounds delighted and we meet in a few days as she was leaving town. I remind her of a remark she made to me some thirty-five years ago. "Thea, you like to write, maybe you should study journalism." I now tell her I'm following her advice of long ago, but it's taken me this long to find the right topic. She laughs! We discussed this writing and at one point she interjects "You have a calling." I leave her with only a promise that she will not be bored.

I wait! Maybe I should not have done this. This cultured woman has done extensive reading and studying. She reads an average of three books a week. She could read my journal in three or four hours. She asked if I was in a hurry. I replied "No, take your time," forgetting how my patience limit is deficient. The day goes by and the next and the next. I wonder what she's thinking as she reads. I notice my tapes from a seminar I attended and wondered if they would help her understand. This speech had helped pull "things" together for me.

My phone rings and the familiar voice says, "It's absolutely marvelous, you write very well." I could have received no greater praise.

I tell her about the tapes and she would like to listen to them. I dropped them off later in the morning. As I talked with her I could tell she had read in great depth. She remarked, "I think the sequence of the format is fine. Did you realize it shows all of your ups and downs as you wrote?" I had not paid attention, I just wrote. She was not finished and would call me next week.

We did not discuss the content in detail. We talked of changing names, etc. Did she think I was uncomfortable to discuss this with her? Maybe slightly. This morning I think of the saying, "no pain – no gain." I can discuss if need be!

But what do I want to do with this? My neighbor hands me a book that lists only publishers and what each handles. She too writes, but of herbs and gardening. Our topics are totally different. I give it back without opening - I'm not ready. Do I want to do this? Our lives could be changed forever. Ray says only MORE people would look at him on the street and give a knowing smile. He is wonderful! He understands my predicament of how this could help so many people, but we would lose our privacy. He also senses a greater power pushing for a decision and of the roads opening along the way.

Maybe I would have it re-typed with corrections and just share it with those I run into. This would be manageable, but I would reach only a few. Maybe that is what is intended? Maybe I should just put it away on a closet shelf and forget it there? Or I could destroy it all and my WHOLE problem would be gone? So many have told me this is a gift to them that I know I can't burn it.

As I look at a flip-over daily calendar for June 11th, it reads, "Be strong and of good courage," Joshua 1:9. Another calendar which was a gift from pastor and his wife regards prayer and for this day it reads. "There is none on earth that live such a life of joy and blessedness as those that are acquainted with this heavenly conversation" (Richard Baxter). Simple! I just pray for the answer. It will come.

The third part of a daily ritual I have established is reading a Lutheran publication "Christ In Our Home" and today it is as follows:

ST. BARNABAS, APOSTLE

If a kingdom is divided against itself, that
kingdom cannot stand. (v.24)

Dr. Johnson spent her career as a psychiatrist in the mental health system of a western state. While she grew up in a Christian home, she left faith behind as she became involved in her scientific studies. Years later she again came to trust Christ because, she said, "the Christian understanding of human beings and their need for redemption is the most credible I've found."

Jesus' opponents sought to attribute his healing powers to his alliance with the forces of evil. But that doesn't make sense, said Jesus. Satan fights against healing, not for it. Even the kingdom of evil isn't divided in its intentions. Jesus' detractors were discredited on this occasion by their illogic.

Faith is filled with mystery, but it is not irrational. We are not asked to suspend reason or common sense to believe in Jesus Christ. On the contrary, God's gift of reason, when open to God's leading, can guide us to even deeper trust as it did for Dr. Johnson.

Lord Jesus, this day take my mind and my heart,
and use them to your glory. Amen.

PRAYER CONCERN: SCIENTISTS

As I read this I think of a *doctor* I know, a psychologist in a mid-western state. Do I know how she feels about there being a supreme being in this universe? I think I do. She is a part of my journey. How does she feel if I decide to actually publish my journal? As my former teacher stated, "Thea, there are two heroines in your writing. One is you and the other Barb Quinn."

June 12

Thoughts

In re-reading my thoughts from May 16th, I had reflected on the May 2nd dream and still had a question about the older woman in my special *Viewmaster*, and what part she played.

I have discussed this with close friends and we are of the same consensus. The older woman with her hands held out as she approached me as if to assist me - has! She had read my work and made recommendations and corrections. She is Joy Arai! I am also struck that she has a daughter by the same unusual name as my own, *Thea*, but she also has another daughter by the name of GRACE, which has come to mean so much to me.

Even with dreams and names God works mysteriously!

Thoughts

In retracing my upward path to total health, I realize there were three main steps.

The first was the CHEMICAL/PHYSICAL component.

I had reached the end of the line that dark December. I had hit bottom. There was nowhere else to go. I sat there bewildered, not caring about my husband, my children, my extended family, friends, the business, or myself. I didn't care if it snowed or if the sun shined. I didn't give a damn! Just leave me alone. I gave up, but something told me to go to a doctor.

The first doctor tried, but they're busy, and I fell through the cracks as they say. I still searched and my final doctor too is a busy man, but first he *listened intently*. He had done his research on various medications he prescribed and he seemed to know which would work for me. He was cautious and I have confidence in him. Physically I feel well.

The second step is PSYCHOLOGICAL.

This next step was difficult for me. I did not want to do this step. But the person I found was patient, kind, trustworthy, and loving in her help. I will always treasure the working relationship we established. Barb gave me the tools. I painfully at times used them, but for the most part the search became intriguing as events, memories, and feelings would unfold.

The third and final step is SPIRITUAL.

This has become the most important component, but without the first two steps I would never have reached this third level. I needed the chemical/physical adjustment to lead me into the psychological area where I could never have gone. I needed to take this new wonder drug, Zoloft, to lift me from the despair I was in. This spiritual element slowly crept back into my life and I was unaware until *things* began to happen and I didn't know why.

I had a *church* background. I had been taught God's rules and teachings. I worked with them some *when I wanted to*. Now HE was working through me. I had observed, as a child and growing up, to just quietly follow the rules and this was what I did. I don't know any religious fanatics and I surely don't want to become one. I firmly believe we find our way to God on our own terms, and by how we were raised. As a conservative Scandinavian Lutheran comfortable with liturgy - I feel I shall remain so. This does not mean this is the only path to God as the roads are many.

I have always spent a great deal of my time enjoying nature. This is God's handiwork. I roamed farm land for years as a child watching nature reproduce and grow. Today I see seeds in my hand go into my garden rows and slowly sprout and grow and this still is amazing to me. They seem so lifeless at first . . . as I felt in *that* December.

I now walk in the woods behind our home and enjoy the trees, the sounds of the birds warning each other of an intruder (they need not fear - they are safe), a chipmunk may dash away and I smile. The damp woodsy odors fill my head and it is peaceful here.

The flowers of spring I love and look forward to. The Trillium, Dutchman's-Breeches, Jack in the Pulpit, Forget-Me-Nots, Yellow Trout Lily and at the wood's edge, Periwinkle. As a child on my walks I would pick a bouquet of flowers and bring them to my mother. We would put them in a glass of water and they would sadly droop. I no longer pick them.

As I said, I heard all of the *teachings* about God, but nature has made me the believer. To have grown up in a county the Indians named *Land of Delight* has been a blessing. The seasons change here and we watch God work his miracles around us daily.

We always welcome spring and can hardly wait for the first signs of robins, bluebirds, and a patch of green. I think of Northport Point as I have been there in spring. This is a season most of the resorters miss which I believe is the most beautiful of all. The abundance of wildflowers, water, and the woods in its many shades of green with large majestic homes rising in a morning haze is breathtaking. The workers enjoy this season as the *Point* comes to life.

Summer comes rapidly some years and we welcome the warmth, the deep blue water, sailboats in the bay, the outdoor picnics and life in general. This is the season we most often hear the locals saying, "A view of the bay is half your pay." We become busy reveling in this season and soon August is here and we are ready. God knows this!

He also has a promise and we know we can expect a color-splashed fall of shortening days. By mid-October we have rested in this glory and ever so often he gives us a summer-like day as a remembrance. Some will say this is Indian Summer, but they argue, "No, we haven't had a touch of snow" (which some call Squaw Winter). These people are still hoping for a few days more of nature's warmth in our future.

The snow begins to fall and we think of Thanksgiving and Christmas. We change our cooking into soups, stew and comfort foods to warm our souls. We use our fireplaces and love the feeling and smells of a home entering winter. We are content. We discuss the color of the caterpillars (will the winter be long - did the caterpillar have a long dark center and light brown ends or was the center short and ends long this fall?). A totally black caterpillar if found could frighten us into not telling others. This could be ominous - Nature knows! We read the almanac as I always seem to buy one. I only read of winter and I wonder, "How bad could it get this season?" Then I realize we are prepared. The fuel oil has been delivered, the freezer and pantry are stocked and we would wait out any storm with our hobbies of baking, reading, carving and watching the storm.

The snow blankets us and tucks us in and we rest. When it seems long and almost endless we remember a promise that God does send spring. It will come!

Spring is here!

Some days it rains in the spring and the earth slows down as we do. This happened to me several weeks ago. I drove into town on an errand and had *slowed* down. As I neared my destination I noticed Jim was painting across the street from where I wanted to go. I approached his truck and he saw me and his eyes lit up and I gave him a hug and a kiss. He said, "I hardly knew you, what happened to you?" I laughed, looked him in the eye and said, "I lost 70 pounds and found God." This just flowed out of my mouth without a second thought . . . what did I say? He smiled and said, "I was just thinking of Jesus and what a beautiful day it is." I needed to run into this man today! (Coincidence?) We talked and it was as if he knew of my struggle with grace and proceeded to give me unsolicited information.

"Find the oldest, wisest person you know and have that person teach you how to say NO!" I protested, "Jim, I have all this energy to share and I can help these people." He said, "Listen, I know but when people find you, and THEY WILL, most of them are lazy and they didn't see your days, nights, weeks, months, or years of struggle. They want a quick fix and they will drain you. It's like an electrical outlet - they will plug in and drain you dry! Know your limits! They will kill you; they see something they want and they want it now!"

I could not believe what he was saying and yet it made sense. I looked at this tall dark Indian with those jet black eyes that I had just hugged and kissed and it came to me. Jim KNOWS because he has grace. I asked him when he first knew and he was fifteen. Wow! I guessed this to be close to thirty years ago. What a source of information. I at fifty-two had *sort of* accepted this grace for only a few weeks.

Jim has GREAT respect for nature. Everything has a purpose and he talks to nature and understands its complexities and is still searching. This man also knows God and it exudes from him. God is mysterious in his works and Jim is mysterious also - he caused me to question and search. I need to do this and I know Jim will be a mentor.

"Here's something else," he said. "When you first meet someone, greet them and just ever so slightly move back. All people are not receptive." He showed me what he meant and I related this to several incidents and meekly said, "OK."

At one point he made me uncomfortable when he said "You are a sacred woman." I didn't deserve to be called this. Only God-like people (popes, priests, ministers, etc.) or places (churches, temples, etc.) are sacred.

My friend Mary and I discussed this topic. She said, "God dwells in us in spirit and we are used to the term *spirit* versus *sacred* which Indians use and are familiar with." "You are God's temple." 1 Corinthians 3:16-17 and 1 Corinthians 6:19.

When Jim first said this to me I thought he misspoke; I was a SCARED woman some days!

He continued, "When you have negative thoughts, feelings, or someone is not receptive, say one-hundred times 'I am a sacred woman' and those feelings will leave you." He was dead serious. I, after several weeks know he is right! It works! I can say one-hundred times, "I am a spiritual person." We all seek the same spiritual destination by the path we are familiar with.

In parting Jim gave me an Indian blessing and said, "Don't EVER WORRY about the right answer — just concentrate on the correct questions." I quickly interpreted that God will always answer in HIS way and I in reverence and wonder began to question.

WHERE WILL THIS LEAD?

As I described, the spiritual component is the most important, and took the longest in my description. Some people complete the first and second step and stay there. I reached the third level by *grace* and being willing to totally accept this *grace* which God freely and continually offers all of us.

Thoughts

My session with Barb yesterday was delightful. Her office was cold so we walked to the Boardman River and sat on the bank. I had always known this park in "Old Towne" was here, but only in passing. I noticed the benches and picnic tables from the road. This find was all new to me in the middle of Traverse City. At first I wondered why she was bringing me here amongst the pipes, railings, and heavy cement structures. It didn't look inviting. I noticed youngsters on a lower level fishing and I asked, "Where can we sit?" "Oh, I know a great spot," she said. We moved further along this maze of cement and pipes running along the ground.

Ahead was a lovely view - a small pond or lake, but not as large as I think a lake should be. A bridge in the distance (part of Cass Street) and two people in a canoe getting ready to fish complete the scene. We sat on a grassy knoll and could look over the pilings into the river.

Barb had been asking me about myself as we walked to this spot and I hedged, *I was fine*. I asked about her motorcycle trip and she told me all about it. They had a great time. "Now, how about you?" I looked at her unsure of what I wanted to tell her. Finally it came, "I think I want to write a book, publish my journal." There, it was out. Would she think this was totally outlandish; that maybe I had more serious mental problems? She smiled, "I know." She did? This was news to me! She knew I was going to do this for sometime, (Joy says probably from page 5) and seemingly just waited for me to announce this. In the next few minutes I told her how she was so much a part of my journey and WE had to see this through together. I explained about the loss of privacy and not wanting to do any harm to those mentioned in my writings.

She remarked, "I'm a pretty low-profile person." I knew why, but I at least had to use her real first name. She consented. We would deal with her name on the cover later. At this point, neither of us had any doubt WE would do this intended book. After it had been placed on the computer she would edit my writing, but she stressed for me to cut nothing. I promised.

We all need assurance in a new venture. I have been getting this from many.

How do I break this news to my mother? She is soon to be eighty-eight and this could be a shock. There is no way I could proceed until I have dealt with this.

This morning when rising I *felt* this is the day, but I stall - I need to be sure. Finally, I decide to say nothing and just take her the paper, which I do most mornings, and check on her. I bring her coffeecake, a neighbor's treat, and we have coffee.

I scarcely tasted my coffee when she said, "I liked the letter you wrote to Harold, (her grandson and my nephew) and your closing is something I do every night." (Give your problems to God, He's up all night anyway.) "If I had not done this I would never have survived living with your father."

WOW! She had never said anything like this to me before. She talked about him and how he would go for days and weeks and not speak. She spoke of his anger and at times how he frightened her.

We discussed many things; the anger in our family and I explained this connection to alcohol. But, I missed something which Ray drew to our attention this evening.

Over dinner the three of us spoke of my father. Ray said simply, "Your father suffered from depression also." As we continued it all made sense. Maybe my grandfather had it also along with the alcohol problem. As I told Harold, it goes hand in hand. How many family members had inherited this trait or gene?

I remember the story of my Aunt Myrtle who died at age thirty-seven, shortly after her own mother died. We recently learned from my uncle that her death had been a suicide. My mother speaks of Myrtle's melancholy and how she liked her.

At the time of my grandmother's funeral my mother offered Myrtle a bedroom at the farm. It was to be hers and she could store things or do whatever she wanted with this space. It would be locked and only she would have the key. She asked, "Do you really mean it?" and when my mother affirmed she went to tell her sisters. The sisters bristled and soon left, along with Myrtle who returned a few months later in a box.

I wonder as I write this - how many of us are there living today, walking around and not knowing what depression is.

I remember another - my cousin and his wife who were killed by a train. They had been stopped, according to witnesses, and as the train approached, pulled onto the track. He always had a fascination for trains and would in younger years, with my Aunt Esther, drive for miles to watch trains. She told this to my sister and me.

My Aunt Esther also had unexplained anger. Even her husband trod softly around her. We never knew how *she* would be when visiting. She could be pleasant and loving or she could hate the sight of anyone.

I wonder of the later generations and how they are doing. Do they know, or, do they think this is normal as I had?

JUNE 15
Thoughts

4:00 a.m.

I've been awake only for a few minutes. Ray uses the bathroom and returns to bed. I hear someone moving in the stillness of the house. Why are we all awake? The thought of Curt and Mark being OK hits my mind. The oldest, Curt, is in the service. Mark left for the Upper Peninsula with a friend to hike and rock climb. "Angels, please guard them" is my thought. It seems too warm to sleep and I get up.

Jon is heating a Pop Tart and I ask, "Why are you up?" He's going to the gym. "Now? It's the middle of the night!" I exclaimed. "They're open twenty-four hours a day and I planned to do this." I make coffee and check the temperature. It's nearly 80 degrees inside and out! This is unusual for this time of year.

I drink my coffee and think of how tired I shall be tomorrow. I think of my mother and of a dream she told me about having the other night. In this dream she is outside by a shed conversing with an older woman. She can't see her face, but knows in her dream this is her mother-in-law who died many years ago. From around the corner a man appears and just stands and watches. He says nothing, makes no movement, but in this dream he is my father. She woke and said this dream bothered her, and she would never forget it.

When she had finished telling me this I asked what *they* were wearing and she replied only dark clothes and she could not see either face, but knew who they were.

As I write this I have a sad feeling and in the morning I need to ask her what time of year did it appear to be in her dream? Did something tell her what time of year it was? Does something tell us in our unconscious or dreams that our *time* is nearly up here, but others we loved are waiting for us? I like this thought.

125

She spoke yesterday of the day I was born. She told me this years ago, but I had forgotten. "I was worried when you were born as you did not cry like the others had - I thought you were dead. There was something over your head which your grandma called a veil, and when it was removed you cried and I knew you were alright." I asked as I had years ago what this would have been? She still didn't know. Then she said, "Your grandma said it was a sign you were especially blessed." (An old wives' tale.)

I think of a song we use at baptisms, weddings and funerals and · how we are *ALL* blessed.

This song moves all of us when we sing it. We feel deeply this belief. Some weep not in sadness, but for joy.

5:00 a.m.

The birds have begun to sing replacing the night sounds of crickets. My day shall be long.

I Was There to Hear Your Borning Cry

I was there to hear your borning cry,
I'll be there when you are old.
I rejoiced the day you were baptized,
To see your life unfold.

I was there when you were but a child,
With a faith to suit you well;
In a blaze of light you wandered off
To find where demons dwell.

When you heard the wonder of the word
I was there to cheer you on;
You were raised to praise the living Lord,
To whom you now belong.

When you find someone to share your time
And you join your hearts as one,
I'll be there to make your verses rhyme
From dusk till rising sun.

In the middle ages of your life,
Not too old, no longer young,
I'll be there to guide you through the night,
Complete what I've begun.

When the evening gently closed in
And you shut your weary eyes,
I'll be there as I have always been
With just one more surprise.

I was there to hear your borning cry,
I'll be there when you are old.
I rejoice the day you were baptized,
To see your life unfold.

John Ylvisaker

JUNE 16
Thoughts

5:30 - 6:00 a.m. Someone touches my shoulder and says quietly, "Mom."

My youngest son Mark, aged twenty, stands by my bed. "I hit a deer with my car. What should I do?" I thank God he's OK! "Why do they never wake the father?" hits my head. But Ray, too, is awake at the sound of Mark's voice.

I walk with Mark and his friend Matt to look at a battered old V.W. which, up until minutes ago, had been his pride and joy. The driver's side in front is badly damaged, but it begins near the center of the hood. The hood is crumpled and askew with hair mixed with bits of glass and metal. Something is dripping on our new asphalt driveway. Both boys speak rapidly explaining the event and how quickly it happened. The adrenalin rush is still flowing and they follow me into the living room. Ray handles their questions, police report, etc.

I sit with them and I feel they are thinking I will chew them out, but I am only thankful they are safe. There will be other cars. I tell them of my thoughts about guardian angels two nights ago when they were in the Upper Peninsula.

They look at one another with a *look* I've become accustomed to after twenty-seven plus years. (Mark has a brother with the same *look*.) They asked what time it was when I had this thought. They were peacefully sleeping on Randy's floor at 4:00 a.m.

Earlier in their exploration they had traveled in a remote area some fifty miles and had questioned their own safety, of car trouble, etc. My thoughts were, "Maybe their angels were early or twenty-six hours late." They may have had the same feeling by the expressions I saw.

JUNE 21

Thoughts

The first day of summer! YES!

I realized at 5:00 a.m. I have missed my writing for several days. My weekend was busy as Chuck and Charlotte visited and I had a great birthday.

June 18th began with John 3:16, a favorite of mine, on the calendar. This was followed by lousy golf with Charlotte and the men. By the beginning of the fifth hole – I filled in our total card for the game. We tied at fifty and finished the round in contentment at how many holes we parred! I read a sign in the clubhouse, "He with the fastest cart has the best lie." Good advice! The men tolerated our antics in good humor with words like "head down, relax, bend knees, eye on ball, water ahead, and poison ivy."

Mother did not feel well on Friday and we were concerned. We have had too hot a day for her. I had a chance to ask her about her dream and what time of year it was. She said "It wasn't winter as it felt warm."

On Sunday we quickly threw together a picnic and ended up with sixteen relatives for dinner, conversation and cards. I don't even remember when we last did this and had such a good time. It had to be close to fifteen years ago as Mark and Jon asked why Uncle Otto and Aunt Betty were here. On Monday several commented on the good time. Mother enjoyed seeing all of us together, harmonious, and perhaps this is why it occurred.

Thoughts

When I think of my youngest son I smile. He was born with charisma and he makes us all laugh. He's a charmer.

As an infant he came home from Munson Hospital with a twinkle in his eye. His grandma said, "He knows our voices, look at him - it's like he can't wait to see what *we* look like instead of us inspecting him."

We think of babies sleeping and not seeing for a few days, but this guy was ready for anything. His brothers took charge and as we placed him on the living room floor they had books to read to him.

Mark is a survivor! He survived being jumped over by his brothers and the Kelty boys on their bicycles as he was part of their ramp! He was hit in the eye with a baseball bat. Mary Peterson would never be available to babysit for them again!

In summer, Mark played with Nate in Allington's pond. They examined every species in the neighborhood. I've wondered if he realized he covered areas where his parents, grandparents, great-grandparents and great-great-grandparents had one time walked and worked. Someday he will know this and it will dawn on him how deep his roots are in Leelanau County. All three sons love our area and are descendants from three different centennial farm families in this county (Kellogg, Solem and Mork).

As a small boy, Mark was a *worry wart*. He never wanted to stay with anyone, even Sharon Phillips, if I had to leave him if only for a short time. The tears would form and spill over and run down his cheeks. At first he had difficulty staying at the Allingtons. He knew he worried! One summer at swimming lessons he had to go with the group from the beach to the bank basement to watch a movie. He hated swimming lessons in the bay and his remark was, "Now I have something else to worry about."

Sandy Lindley, when I saw her a few weeks ago, reminded me of another Mark story. She says, "I think of Mark and tell people about his experience with kindergarten round-up when I read about it every spring."

Mark and I had gone to register him for school in the spring and he wasn't crazy about this new venture! The school season went fairly well, I thought. He made new friends, had kids over to play, etc. One night as I read the paper I remarked, "Oh they're having kindergarten round-up next week." His comment I remember well and smile. "I'm glad we don't have to go through that again." He assumed his school days were over and we could get back to normal days at home together.

Mark survived a serious illness at age ten. He became ill in September with allergy-type symptoms. He was hospitalized locally and we were told to take him to Mott Children's Hospital in Ann Arbor. We were informed he had a virus (this means they didn't know either) and by the time he was taken to Mott we were dealing with after effects or side effects. Everyone we knew prayed, cried, supported him and prayed some more. There were times when we didn't think he would live and neither did he. Children died while we were at Mott and he knew this, all the other kids knew this too.

During the four months we were in Ann Arbor, Mark was allowed to go home for three days at Christmas. Friends and neighbors cleaned my house, put up the tree, shopped for food, baked wonderful treats and they too prayed. After Christmas the same group returned –took down the tree, etc. What a wonderful gift of love this was for all of us.

Mark recovered completely except for one small tremor in his right hand when he is extremely tired.

Mark is very artistic and sort of knows where he is headed. He does not fully apply himself as there are many distractions at age twenty. Friends, hiking, biking, skiing, cliff climbing, work and girls.

He loves his job at The Happy Hour Tavern and has worked there for six years. He started washing dishes and is now a bartender which he handles with an artistic flair. The Fischers are like family to him. Yes, I smile when I think of Mark.

Jon, in two months, has come a long way. He takes responsibility for himself and his actions. He is taking control of his life and has a sense of direction. Yes, there is a God!

In the past days I have thought much about my children. What effects did my illness have on them? I'm not sure I know this answer. I find comfort in the fact that they are all finding their way in life and finally seem to be on the right path. Did I have to find my path before they could find theirs? All my children are caring, friendly, loving, funny, creative, protective, sensitive, good listeners, willing to help others and forgiving. If I have ever hurt them I know they will forgive me.

I just realized the words I used to describe my children are some of the very same they used to describe me when I began therapy.

Children learn from our words to them, but I think our example as we go through life has a much greater effect. Some of us and our offspring:

> *"in a blaze of light wander off to find where demons dwell."*

But:

> Through many dangers, toils, and snares,
> We have already come;
> 'Tis grace hath brought us safe thus far,
> And grace will lead US HOME.

I feel my children will be safe while on their journey.

JUNE 24

Thoughts

I have a friend, of many years, Maxine. She has cancer. I hate this damned disease.

As children we played together on farm land - on the hill tops and in ditches where great weeping willows grow. Our secret culvert is much smaller when I stoop to enter now. The water still trickles through it as it did those years before. Our hills are filled with houses soaking up *our* view.

We rode horseback over this land with Shirley who died an early death. She was a free spirit. We felt it at the time. She couldn't be slowed in life and lived it fast and to the fullest. I think of her at Martinson Funeral Home, in her cowgirl boots. She looked at peace, but ready-dressed for her next adventure. She always led the way.

Max and I traveled through weekly Sunday School, Vacation Bible School and were confirmed together.

I watched as she jumped rope and played with others at the old stone school. She knew the games as her sisters taught her well. Sometimes we ate our lunch together on a window seat. We laughed and talked, and wondered as the town friends went home to eat.

We never did the crazy things I did with many others. She would laugh and say, "My God, *how could you?*" as she does today. She questions me and is concerned now as she was then. She gives me food for thought!

At some point we parted closeness, but we asked and thought about each other through family and friends over the years.

When I heard she was ill I didn't want to see her this way. I sent her cards and a pocket cross (the kind we carry to remind us).

Then I saw her at Clyde's (her brother-in-law) funeral and her gentle smile, her caring ways, and great sense of humor all came back to me. I had missed this person!

We lunched, we talked, and we laughed. We discussed her treatment and she is feeling better, looking better and maybe God has answered our prayers in the way we wanted Him to as this is His will also.

Her very close friend says, "Max lives one day at a time. She enjoys the good ones and rides out the not so good." I think, "Don't we all?"

I no longer worry about Max as I know in talking to her she is in good hands everyday and hereafter!

June 27
Thoughts

Pastor Paul phoned to let me know he would like to drop by tomorrow. I wonder what he wants to talk about. Ray will be here.

Thoughts

Paul had heard about my book as his wife and friends of mine have read it. He was curious and had many questions.

I smiled to myself at some of his questions which he asked, and thoughts he expressed. We spoke for almost three hours. He was careful as if walking on eggshells so everything came out as it was intended.

The tension broke when he asked, "Are you still on medication?" I laughed and replied, "Yes, but that's not it!" I had asked Barb this same question myself earlier. Ah Ha! I was ahead of him! He tried to put these words back in his mouth to re-formulate them. I still laughed as he did not seem to understand and I was almost amazed. Then I thought, no, he's amazed and is searching. He spoke of how this possibly would fit in to benefit the church. I had not thought of this. I was only delighted in my own found treasure.

My God, would I have to do something openly? People I know would really think I was some *religious nut*.

Paul left and I tried to figure the whole picture out and I can't. It's just too big!

Letter

Dear Paul,

Thank you for a special ministerial visit yesterday. As I take your words of advisement, the following comes into my mind this morning.

GRACE !
As I set my sights toward heaven,
And give God my all control.
The road expands in my horizon.
Oh, how I feel it in my soul!

The sun seems so much brighter,
As it rises and I know;
That God is there to lead me.
Oh, how I feel it in my soul!

I seem to know the tasks before me,
And I do them with God's Grace!
There no longer is a question,
I shall meet God face to face!

This grace has so much power,
And it moves me with God's care.
I follow grace with all clear vision,
I know that God is there!

We each have our own favors,
By God we have been blest.
Sometimes we need to find these gifts,
And let God do the rest!

I praise my God and worship Him
For I have found my role.
I thank Him for His blessings.
Oh, how I feel it in my soul!

Love,

Thea

Thoughts

Paul asked after church if he could publish the poem I gave him. After much thought, I gave it to the church and they can do whatever they would like with it. It was a gift to me and if others enjoy it, this is fine.

I spoke with Debbie and she read the poem. She does not fully understand the meaning of the poem but says, "Whatever works for you is great." She smiled and said, "You look like you know a secret and you're not telling anyone — it shows in your eyes and face." I only smiled at this friend of a few months.

Debbie and Grace

Debbie thinks I know a secret.
    But, It is there for all to treasure.
It is so difficult to accept It.
    But, It gives such endless pleasure.

I see the old time picture,
    Of Him knocking on the door.
His patience has no limit,
    And His love's forever more!

The gift He gave me freely,
    And I know that It is grace.
But, Debbie looks at me in wonder,
    Or she just stares off in space.

She does not grasp the meaning,
    But, she knows something is there.
Debbie thinks I know a secret,
    That I'm not about to share.

I look at her bewildered,
    She has heard the story well!
She even reasons the existence
    Of a heaven and a hell!

As I look back down my pathway,
    Then turn my head toward home.
I realize in an instant
    I received grace on my own!

Grace is there and freely given,
    Debbie, open up the door!
Debbie thinks I know a secret,
    It's no secret anymore!

Time

As I sit in my back yard and wonder
    Amidst tall trees and misty rain.
Where, Oh where did all the time go?
    I need to find it and reclaim.

I see these majestic trees as infants,
    Struggling in new seeded grass.
We all grew up together
    As the time just seemed to pass.

The sandpile which held such joy,
    Is gone - we now feed birds.
Where flowers grow and roses bloom
    The hunting dogs were heard.

The myrtle grows profusely along the
    Wooded edge.
Where, Oh where did all the time go?
    Keeps entering my head.

"Take time to smell the flowers"
    We were told along the way.
For time goes oh so swiftly
    We heard our elders say.

We listened, but we did not hear,
    As those years flew quickly past.
Where, Oh where did all the time go?
    I still feel I have to ask.

If I could just reclaim one precious moment,
    I don't know which it would be.
Perhaps I know where time goes,
    It's safely clutched in memory.

RED PAINT

I stopped by the paint crew on Setterbo Road
    As they set their equipment to spray.
A man slowly walked to my car window
    And waited for me to say:

"When you get to my house could you put
        Red Hearts
    In the center of the road?"

He smiled, thought, and said "I have no red paint."
    He only had black, white, and yellow.
He turned to his crew as I drove on my way,
    For a moment they had one more color!

July 8

Thoughts

I wrote to M. Scott Peck and asked if he could assist in finding a publisher.

I'm sure he is busy, but maybe he will take the time.

Letter

Dear Otto, Betty, and Darwin,

In December, a year and a half ago, I was diagnosed as having depression which was serious. With the help of a miracle medication, a wonderful doctor, another psychologist with a doctorate degree, family, and friends, I am recovering. This has been a long and sometimes painful process.

I have learned a great deal in the past eighteen or nineteen months about depression. I can recall five different occasions when this *monster* visited me. The last was the worst. I could do nothing – not even the simplest of things.

The most alarming discovery I found is that this disease can be hereditary. It does not affect every family member, but we need to be aware of its existence. If you know of family members that fit any of the following descriptions they may be a candidate for a serious depression someday. I think they can be helped ahead of time by being made aware and seeking the proper help.

Attached is a list of signs and symptoms of depression itself when it hits. I had everyone of these!

1. Moody and unhappy sometimes and don't know why.
2. Some days we talk to people - some days we pretend we don't know them.
3. We have material things - life sucks!
4. We look for gratification in alcohol, drugs, wild times, etc.
5. Irritable to others without cause.
6. Won't talk to people for periods of time.
7. Thoughts of suicide, or clues, or actual plans.

The list goes on.

One of the most important parts of my recovery was keeping a journal of dreams, thoughts, memories, feelings, etc. and sharing it with my psychologist. My writing started out with helping myself, then others with depression or other problems read it. These strangers and I just seemed to find each other. My work has let them know they are not alone with these problems and there is help available. This writing like topsy just grew and I am compelled to write and share. This will come as a surprise to you, but this work is coming off a computer, being edited by my doctor and we are searching for a publisher. When it has been edited, if you wish, you may read it.

Attached is a short piece about Andy and Bob to show you the flavor or type of writing I do. You know them so well I thought this might be fun. Enjoy!

Love,

Thea

Love Is

Love is in funny things. It's waking in the middle of the night or early morning and having to use the bathroom. We have a family joke - we call each other on the phone or say to our bed-partner, "Don't you have to *go?*" They instantly hate us, ignore us, smile and get out of bed! We are content — *Gotcha!*

Love is seeing a tired mother at eighty-eight years return from playing in a kitchen band and handing her a tall drink. She tries to enjoy a movie we are watching, but falls asleep.

Love is seeing a nephew and watching his eyes light up as he talks. Sometimes we say nothing - it's a glance and a grin. We know what the other is thinking. We are soul mates.

Love is in this nephew's children. These two boys telephone me, "May we visit?" They are nine and eleven and arrive on small motorcycles. I love to hear them coming through the orchards and fields. They always check my cookie jar - sometimes the bigger boys have beaten them to it. Their bottom lips stick out in humor, but I usually have other treasures to eat.

Love is doing fun things together. We pick blueberries in the rain at Buchans, sometimes go to movies, visit the bookstores, try each other's food when we eat out and we all like breakfast best. We no longer visit the zoo - we feel sorry for the caged animals on hot pavement pacing. We think of their fear at Festival when the Blue Angels fly over. They too should be free.

These two have talents. They work with wood and give me gifts. I have elephants, turtles, snowmen, ghosts, and ducks, etc. These presents are priceless as they are made with love. They do well in school, they rank high in Karate, are card sharks, pool sharks and I won't teach them golf.

We explore! We three like to try new ventures and value each other's thoughts. We range in age from nine to fifty-three, but we meet in the middle and share. They ask me questions and I'm truthful to them in answers. Sometimes *we* need to look answers up as their questions are profound. They give me innocence and I marvel if only this could just stay with them. They like undivided attention and they know I *listen* to each of them. We trust each other and would never laugh *at* each other but we laugh *with* each other.

I love the expressions they use and their humor. I wrote a poem about having a paint crew put hearts in the center of the road in front of my house. They liked this poem. We look at the road when we return from our ventures and Bob says, "They still haven't been back." We all three hope they will come.

Recently they phoned me as they were home alone and a thunderstorm came up. "Could you come and get us?" After we

145

made cookies we headed to The Happy Hour for lunch. On the way I asked, "If I wasn't home this morning who would you have called?" They didn't know. I assured them it was OK to be frightened as it was a terrible storm, but sometimes people we depend on can't always be there (parents work, grandparents are away, aunts are not always home, the phone goes out, etc.). One of them, I think Andy, said, "Sometimes they even die like Uncle Clyde." I caught my breath and said, "Yes, but God is always there and we can always rely or call on Him when we are in trouble. I call Him." I will always remember Bob's reply, "I bet that's a heck of a phone bill."

These two grandnephews speak often of *Uncle Clyde*. This was their first funeral of someone very close to them. He always had time for them and shared of himself. They know their daddy misses his partner in work and play. They want to know about funerals; What happens to a body? "Do you think Uncle Clyde looks the same today as when we put him in the ground? Does a body smell? I bet it does." These questions are endless and I know they wonder about themselves and their own mortality. I try to reassure their Catholic teachings as basically these teachings are my own. We are all Christians. "Uncle Clyde, as we knew him, is not in that body - his spirit has left it and waits for us and someday you will both see him again in heaven which has no end." They like this answer and are comforted by God's promise. They surprise me as they tell me they think I am different and they like me going to church.

We talk, as we ride, of relatives and how they are related to the Kalchik family, but I am not. We decide one of our new ventures is to make them a family tree. Bob grumbles, "I suppose I will be by the roots as I'm the youngest." Yes Bob, all trees need fresh tender roots.

I have a magnet on my fridge - it's an apple with a place for a picture. Andy's photo has been here for nearly all of his eleven years. He is my Godson and he would on occasion have to remind Bob of this special place he held. Bob hates this magnet! He fiddles with it often and usually leaves it upside down. I need to explain when next they come and see the magnet that it's been added to. When Andy was first born, I was chosen to be his Godmother and I can't change this, nor would I want to. But, I can choose to add Bob to my list of Godchildren and think of him as such. I put both their names in the magnet.

These two little boys are growing and soon will become young men. They won't be able to visit as often and will venture on new paths. I shall enjoy watching them discover and grow and stay in touch by lunches, or just maybe a breakfast at Sweitzers and Bob can sample my cherry pancakes when he has ordered plain ones.

These two are full of wonderful thoughts, love, promise, and a hope for the Mork family future as are all of this generation. I wish I had taken the time to know all the nieces and nephews as I know these two. We all lost!

———————————

Thoughts

I was the reader in church yesterday for the first time and was struck by one line in the reading.

> *"My grace is sufficient for you,*
>   *for power is made perfect in weakness."*
> 2 CORINTHIANS 12:7-10.

July 15
Thoughts

What do I put on the cover of this book? What is the title going to be?

I keep returning to photos of the beach at Gulf Shores. They show a beautiful sunset that seems to go on forever.

I tell Ray, "There're sunsets on my book cover. Maybe all five in a row like in my dream of April 18th." He replies, "Are you sure in the dream it wasn't sunrises?"

I read the dream aloud and he has a look of "I know what it is!" He leaves the room!

I look at the dream again in disbelief. I see it — it's there! The five sunsets all in a row are my siblings and myself. As I make my journey to the top, my sister and brothers join me on the way as I allow them to read the book. At the very top we are in a row of agreement because we all know this book will benefit our family and many others. It is so simple. Some of them moved quickly when I told them about the book. They thought of their children and grandchildren and how this could help them. Two have not read the book yet, but I know in time they will.

My neighbor, Clayton, suggests the sunsets represent five major steps in my recovery.

1. I see there is a problem finally and recognize it.
2. I know the problem could be difficult as the tower is high and the road is winding and tough.
3. I seek the help of three doctors eventually and the medication works.
4. As difficult as it was, I went for psychological help.

5. On this crooked and steep road I needed God and He was there.

Maybe there are as many interpretations as there are readers. I like both of the above.

My mother has read the book and commented, "We are a well-known family in Leelanau, but we do what we have to do." She always has!

The title comes to me as I look at these photos. My family and I have *New Horizons???*

July 19
Thoughts

In the past few days I have dealt with people and their problems. I will not write about them. I will not break their confidence. It is tiring to think of them all of the time. I need to be able to *let go* of them after they talk.

July 21

Thoughts

I am tired, I am doubting my ability to write anything. Maybe this is all just a wild hyped-up ego trip. My day yesterday was just too full. I did too much. I think of my Indian friend Jim, and what he warned me of – "they will plug in and drain you dry."

Katie had written me a letter and I was concerned about her. She is one of millions of young adults who think they know so much, but don't know where they are going. They think of a safe time in their life (if they ever had one) and they reminisce as if they are eighty years old. They know they have to make a decision because all of a sudden high school is over and they, for the first time in their lives, are asking, "Now what do I do?"

Peer pressure took me to college along with a desire to please my parents. This was thirty-five years ago. I became a teacher because everyone else I knew was becoming one. As I look around and think of my close college friends - none of us are teachers. We taught school briefly and then drifted to other areas.

I reread Katie's letter and she has had great tragedy for someone so young. She has suffered losses and blames herself. She needs something to hang onto. I worry about her as I have come to love her. Katie is not her real name, but I use this name as it is what we would have named the daughter we never had.

Later I saw my *computer genius*. We talked of the book, layout, other more complicated things.

I should have quit for the day. But, it was only 9:00 a.m.

I follow through on another road to open doors for a future encounter. This lovely young person too needs help, but in another way. She's so positive she knows God. She missed the first two steps and she needs a doctor and some psychological help. It will come.

In returning to the bookstore, my dreams of self-publishing are smashed. "Don't go there." I hear from two who should know. People are having problems with them. I will check out the rumor.

By noon I had taken Mother for a doctor's appointment and spoken to someone about a relative with problems.

At 1:30 I headed for Traverse City with a long list; drug store for Mother, pick up book from Barb as she finished editing, go to Northwestern Michigan College bookstore, pick up copy of book which was being read by friends (not home), went to second bookstore to look for books by Morton Kelsey (none).

No breakfast - yogurt lunch!

At 3:00 I grocery shop as we are having company. I call Ray and tell him I'm on my way with groceries from hell — let's eat out.

Over dinner Ray tells me of a strange phone call. A former customer and friend phoned to ask if we were both OK. She had a premonition and had thought of us for several days.

I looked at Ray and felt impending doom. My God - Do we eat and die on the way home? I should have had something evil for dessert instead of Caesar Salad!

At home I try to read and relax. I still think of the premonition. I look over Barb's editing and I think, "Why am I doing this?"

Two families reading the book haven't called. I'm tired, but I squeeze in a double batch of black raspberry jam.

It's 9:30 p.m. and I phone the friend with the premonition. Oh yes, she has these at times and just had to check on us. She shares the fact that her mother has depression and is on medication. She mentions several others and says, "It is everywhere." I agree and hang up still wondering if I should have had that dessert.

Again, I think of Jim saying "know your limits" and realize I pushed myself too far.

I read today's reading which is based on the 23rd Psalm and it tells of goodness and mercy, but it also reminds me "He restoreth my soul."

Thoughts

My book has been read by many. I search for the next step while those who read offer suggestions. They have titles, ideas of how to publish, make this clearer, add this word. Usually I listen! Some edit, type, proofread or encourage and I just read where someone wrote it takes more than one person to write a book. Friends suggest titles involving the sunsets. My computer genius has solved our title search with *Visions of Sunsets*.

July 24

Dream

In this dream I am shopping and I see a newspaper stand. There is a man calling out the headlines. I only hear part of his voice as there are cars and traffic noise. I don't know where I am, but I'm OK.

As I get closer I see the whole front page. There is a headline involving God. I think how amazing that God should make the headlines when we only read of tragic things (murder, drugs, wars, famine, crooked politics, etc.).

I decide to buy this paper as I also see the name **M. Scott Peck** and his picture. There's an article about Rwanda, etc.

I look at the article on God. It's from Sault Ste. Marie and was picked up by Associated Press. It tells of a religious order that had been made up of people from different walks of life living in a commune-type setting in the Upper Peninsula. It had failed. The article told of their character, morals, life style, and how they had used God wrongly. They were disbanding.

It was not a happy headline after all!

Attached to each newspaper was a small plastic bag divided in the center. It had a ribbon and bow to hold it shut. The top half held dark-looking seeds with instructions, "Do Not Plant!" The bottom seed packet looked like a mixture of wildflower packets and it was larger. I thought, "I will scatter these seeds in my new wildflower field in front of the house."

The story had told how when this religious cult had failed it still had money left over. They had packaged these seeds to be given away free. They were stapled to the newspaper. There were instructions on their care, as if done by Burpee Seed Company:

"Open carefully as seeds are small. Simply scatter in area desired for seeds to root and new growth should occur. No need to cover as they have been provided for. Nature will in time, multiply (perennials) and their beauty will be ten times ten. Height and color will vary. *Minimum care required*."

I look at the section where the article was on **M. Scott Peck**. It's gone and I cannot find it. I search frantically as I want to read about him and where he is. It's gone and I wake.

JULY 24

Thoughts

As I'm awake I decide to make coffee and read daily messages.

FIRST READING

" I sought to hear the voice of God and climbed the topmost steeple.
But God declared, "Go down again, I dwell among the people."
Author Unknown

I think of the song which has a line "looking for love in all the wrong places." Or maybe I've been looking in the wrong places for a publisher. Maybe it's not M. Scott Peck on the mountain of publishers. Maybe it's among those I find along the way.

SECOND READING

SUNDAY JULY 24   MARK 6:30-34

NINTH SUNDAY AFTER PENTECOST
" He said to them, 'Come away to a deserted place all by yourselves and rest a while.'" (v.31)

Workaholics are more common than alcoholics.
Even in a society that constantly promotes recreation, hobbies, and travel - like the United States - most people work hard and long. Even retired folk often say that if they were busier they would have to hire a helper.
We have a lake cottage in northern Minnesota where there are comparatively few people. Though it takes a certain amount of work to keep up such property, it is still restful to get away for a while to different, less demanding surroundings.
Perhaps the greatest error, if not sin, in respect to resting today is improper use of the day Christians have set aside as the Lord's Day. To worship God in community with other believers, to pray, and to spend time in simple rest and in attention to relationships too often yields to shopping, doing laundry, or dashing off to activities.
Jesus' words remind us of what God did on the seventh day: God rested on the seventh day and hallowed it.

Almighty God, we confess our faults. Help us
keep the seventh day your hallowed day.
Amen

WEEKLY PRAYER CONCERN: NATIONS AT WAR

I think of how tired I was on Wednesday and the after effects
which are somewhat with me. I would have done laundry this
afternoon as I have more company coming Tuesday. It can wait!

THIRD READING

ACCEPTANCE/HUMILITY   JULY 24

*'But if you go and ask the sea itself, what does it say? Grumble,
grumble, swish, swish. It is too busy being the sea to say anything
about itself.'*
                                        Ursula K. Le Guin

No one who has ever sat beside the sea and experienced
her eternal power and gentleness can have any question that
the sea knows that she is just that, the sea. Nature has such an
ability to be exactly what she is, with no pretense. . . and she
does not even have to stop and think about it.

When we have to stop and think who we are, we are not
being who we are. When we are trying to be someone we
believe we should be, we are not being who we are. When we
are trying to be what someone else has told us we should be,
we are not being ourselves. To be myself, I have to be.

Nature teaches great lessons in humility. In order to learn from
her, I have to be in her.

I have enjoyed the past few months of just being me!

FOURTH READING

*" The call to grace is a promotion, a call to a position of higher
responsibility and power." p. 301*
                The Road Less Traveled, M. Scott Peck

I think of my dream and all four of these readings and how each
is entwined in my life.

July 26 & 27

Thoughts

I think of this illness of depression and how awful it is. To be so far down and so low that I thought of suicide terrifies me today.

The thought of going off my Zoloft in September causes great apprehension. I feel so well, safe and content that a phrase crosses my mind. "If it ain't broke – don't fix it."

Barb has assured me if I need to, I can keep taking Zoloft. I will try stopping this medication for a time as a trial period. I will know if I am *slipping* and phone my doctor.

How wonderful for scientists to have discovered this medication. Where would I be without it?

I think of watching the TV talk shows and how I was swayed by their presentation. If others on medication were watching, I hope they also found their way back if they stopped taking their miracle drug.

I must learn to slow down and limit myself. I don't want another July 20th in my life. It took this day to draw my attention to what I was doing to myself. I did this all my life. I needed to be slowed down. I have learned in my encounters with others that their problems are their own to solve. I cannot carry their burdens, but I can point out the pathways where they can seek help. I hope this book helps give them courage to seek their own journey.

There are parts of my journey that I don't like, but they can't be ignored as they are part of the whole picture. This was my journey through depression and others may be entirely different.

Our lives are like our fingerprints, no two are alike. We each carry our own *baggage* and when it gets too heavy we hit bottom.

Sometimes we wallow in this pit because as stubborn people *in control* we think we should be able to handle it — ourselves. We don't want to be dependent on anyone or anything. Even God!

A day arrives and we discover there are problems we just can't handle alone. I finally went to three physicians, a psychologist, read books, attended seminars, etc. Then Dr. Meg Meeker's words hit me "You need to understand the source of your anger - if you can't identify it, give it to God. He knows it anyway." She termed these next steps the 4 - F's:

1. First give it to God or Come to God.
2. Figure out your anger.
3. Focus and walk through your anger.
4. Forgiveness (forgive those who angered you and you will be restored).

This works!

Two lines come into my mind.

"God gives us what we can handle and not a measure more. He's always there to guide us *if* we open up the door!"

As I look to the future, I know there will be ups and downs in my life. Life has hills and valleys for everyone. I also know that God is here *doing his thing*. I have seen His work in my life, through Nature's beauty, my dreams, my writing, coincidences (there are none - He is at work), people I have encountered searching for him, and the list goes on.

He works mysteriously for all of us and I thank Him for His blessings and His grace.

Abyss / Hope

We think we know this person, we know her oh so well.
But deep within this being, we know not what does dwell.
The pain, the shame, the anger, she carried through the years.
She never knew why it was there, she only shed the tears.

She knew not what the reason the turmoil churned inside.
She knew not what the season it choose to in abide.
She only knew the presence and felt it to the core.
She had to rid this demon so it would come no more.

She chose the road less traveled, was enlightened on the way.
The road became much smoother as she traveled day by day.
The mountain top was reached, she did it with His aid.
For God was there beside her, His promise had been made.

She now must tell the others, it's there for all to share,
When we ask for God to help us, He keeps us in his care.
I love this God and worship Him. I find Him everywhere!
I see Him in a tiny seed and in great love I share!

JULY 28

Thoughts

I know not where this little book is going, but I know I'm going to love the ride.

I woke at 5:00 a.m. and wrote the poem rapidly. This was a sad, but yet happy poem. I think about the poem and the above thought for a few minutes. I remember a dream of March 27th. I smile and then laugh. I know the meaning . . . *it's pretty obvious who's driving the bus*.

AUGUST 2

Thoughts

I awake this morning and think of my feelings. Yesterday was a day with free time on my hands. I enjoyed this. The day just passed uneventful and after days of company it was welcome.

As I glance at lace curtains moving in the breeze, I think this is how I feel. The breeze is gentle, and if an open book were lying here its pages would slowly move and turn. They may move in either direction depending on the mood of the wind. They may not move at all, but still feel the breeze flow over and move on.

I think of Barb's question yesterday when she phoned. "How are you doing?" "I'm fine." This came out automatic and I do feel OK. She has asked me this question before and it is not just in passing. There is a change in the inflection of her voice and tone. She is usually upbeat and quick, but when she asks this question there is concern in her voice and something else. Sort of like, "Don't just say you're fine, but think about your answer."

This is my answer.

It dawns on me. I am the book and I am now open. This breeze is everyday life and today it gently moves me. The sun is shining and birds are singing.

I have weeds in my garden - t a l l weeds. There is furniture to refinish for a friend, but she is patient. She has waited two months and gave up asking. She has watched me slow down and likes this. But not at all cost! This friend does too much - it is amazing how I see this now. I think of all the projects I had going at one time and I smile. A smile of relief that my grass is too tall and my house needs cleaning.

I would rather *just listen* to Ray or the boys and hear things I never heard before. Then bake them a fat-free pie with a criss-cross crust and enjoy the smiles.

Or I could play with Andy and Bob and return to being a nine and eleven year old and enjoy the world through their eyes. It is easy for me now to just slip into their world and be comfortable. It is like exploring the same questions I had at their age. Their world is much different than mine was so many years ago. In most ways I would not want to exchange this time. Leelanau County was ours and we didn't have house keys or locks. We drove aimlessly on Sunday rides in this county and my parents knew everyone and where they lived. I tested them and they knew! A newcomer was a stranger for a good twenty years and then we gave thought that they might remain.

A page turns. Sometimes I question how different I have become. Will this last? How can one individual change so much in attitude, behavior and body and still be the same person? I think of the word phenomenal! This is how I feel!

Old friends or acquaintances I now meet are stunned! Some do not know me at first glance. Then they know it is me, but I'm different. I know I'm different and I smile!

I've lost between sixty and seventy pounds. I walk. I feel much better physically. I have dealt with psychological garbage and it's in a book which before I would have closed and shelved. Now, I search to publish this for anyone to read. We all have some garbage to sort through. Mine is not different from millions of others. I thought it was when I looked into the bag, but not anymore. We all have different bags.

I have thought about self-publishing my journal. The cost is high and could be risky. Then I think I still would control this book. If this book helped but just one person look for help in the right places it would be worth the risk. Ah Ha! I have changed! This is the meaning of "'tis better to give than receive." Tell me this when I was nine or eleven or forty.

My voice is the same (I think) but the words that fall out are much more mellow. When we are open - we become accessible. The large guard in my doorway is gone. People have discovered they can travel in and out of my being. If they see something they like, please use it, take, pass it on to others, it just keeps growing. I like this open book!

A new page! I still have an apprehension that Barb and I have discussed. The time is getting nearer for me to try a separation from my miracle drug. Barb thinks I will be fine without it. I can always go back to it if the need arises. SIMPLE?

A 100% Norwegian is known worldwide to be stubborn, unreasonable, but usually *right*. This Norwegian thinks I feel the best I have felt in my entire life! I take this miracle drug and *if it ain't broke — don't fix it*. I am safe! I got rid of the garbage in my head. Thank you!

What if I do need this drug forever and maybe it won't work as well next time? I do not ever want to go back to the pit! The thought is not a welcome one.

Also, I do not want my journal to harm anyone. I have uneasy moments. Family members may have different memories than mine. They may not like what I have written. I think my sister would like me to shelve this journal. She is glad I am well, but put it away now. My one brother and his wife say "print the book." They see the need to do so.

I have nephews and nieces that find themselves here. A favorite nephew, Ken, says, "I find myself on almost every page."

There are too many closed books in this world. I have discovered by being open I gain much more by hugs than clubs. There is no need to wander in the wilderness when there are green pastures within the book!

Thoughts

Upon awaking I feel down, but it is raining. I phoned my computer genius about a poem. She too is down today as is a friend of hers. *The Genius* has been down a month! Oh no.

She would not go to breakfast to take a break, but will call me later. She is too busy.

Ruth calls and there is no golf today. I have missed three weeks for different reasons.

My readings today were not inspiring except the one on forgiveness of others and how this restores us.

The boys, Andy and Bob, were lonely yesterday and I went to them so they could play in the pool. They are alone too much.

I think I shall call them for breakfast and spend the day with them. I need a nine and eleven year old to talk to – they are so ALIVE. We shall lift each other up!

Move it, use it, or lose it!

dream lost

>   a dream within a dream
>   flowing in the dark
>   the thoughts forever lost
>   gone as vacant as the air
>   embodied in vacuum
>   to flow through
>   canyon walls as a river
>   i cannot see or touch
>   my mind awakens
>   'tis lost forever
>   gone beyond forever
>   in the night.

My Son

My son, My son, My son,
   It's three a.m. I cry!
I realize a grave misdeed.
   I did not let you fly.

Before your birth I loved you!
   I will love you evermore!
'Tis time for you to disembark.
   I shall remain on shore.

When you were small, I held your hand,
   I rocked you in the night.
I watched you grow to a young man.
   I just held on too tight.

As I am healing in my world,
   May you heal and grow in yours.
For I know of open space,
   There are no more closed doors.

The world has opened up for me,
   As I pray it will for you.
You're young - Go do what you love best.
   To your own self be true.

May God always be with you,
   As you travel on your way.
My son, My son, My son,
   You've new horizons on this day!

Love,

Mom

Sunday

Communion, my love, and Mozart
        Did wile away my day.
Will my grace return, will my soul restore?
        How long will I be this way?

The rains did come, this valley reached.
        I slid from the mountain high!
I yearn for the sight of a hilltop,
        I ask my God, "Oh, Why?"

Thoughts

Why did I reach this depth? Is this part of a cycle? Did the Zoloft lose its magic? When did I start to fall? Did the rainy summer bring me here? Did my reading of coincidence question God's grace? Did he dump me here for reflection? Stupid, don't question me again!!!

My *computer genius* smiled, "Welcome to the club." She knows hers comes and goes. But I thought mine was gone for good?? I don't *want* returning down times. "Shake hands" she said, "and make friends with *IT*, these times will come and go. They will get easier when you deal with them and talk to the helper you know."

Thoughts

My week has been one of uneasy feelings. I had not known this *devil*, as I have so named my depression, would return. I thought with my medication, my mind delved into, and a stronger faith, all would be right with my world.

My appointment (Monday, August 8th at 4:15 p.m.) was timely as twelve hours earlier I awoke with tears in the night and not knowing why. These tears just flowed and could not be stopped.

In a torrential downpour of my own and weather-wise, I drove to Sharon, my *computer genius*. With coffee, her caring, her knowledge gained from ?? years of therapy and over eight years in a twelve-step support group, I finally learned as fact what I suspected. "Oh yes, it will reoccur, but never as bad, and never as long or longer. My life goes on and when *it* comes, I just think, 'Oh, it's depression talking' and I deal with it. I recognize the signs and you will too. It gets easier to deal with as time goes on."

In Barb's office I discussed this with her. After a welcomed hug, she reinforced Sharon's comments. "Yes, it may return, but you now have tools to work with and you know it will leave. You have expanded your field of support with family and friends and I'm only a phone call away." She was right (as usual) and I felt comfortable leaving her office without a scheduled appointment in my future.

I do have a complete circle of physical, psychological, and spiritual strength to draw upon. As Barb stated in her prologue to this book, the balance is delicate as well as intricate. By realizing and using all three components I can draw from each of them as I travel through the rest of my life.

My turn to dance with the *devil* may come, but with my doctors, my family, friends, and God's grace. . . *may the waltzes in my life be ever so long and mellow.*

Family Bonds

Family bonds hold tight.
"Blood is thicker than water."
"Don't disgrace the family name."
"You're well, it doesn't matter."

Family bonds hold tight.
   "We're well known and respected."
Leave black depression hidden
      And alcohol not inspected.

Family bonds hold tight.
      I feel their message deep.
Family bonds hold tighter
      The secrets that we keep.

I placed it on the table.
      Some gave it back to me.
They said, "It never happened."
      But, then why am I free?

This family has grown huge.
      It's spread both far and near.
If members are in turmoil,
      There is hope that they must hear.

Family bonds hold tight.
      Family diseases do affect us.
But, what I learned and now must share,
      They do not have to rule us.

Love,

Thea

173

EPILOGUE

When first going public with *Visions of Sunsets*, there were times I felt naked or exposed. My life had been gone over with a fine tooth comb. I waded and sifted through nearly fifty years of memories, experiences, and feelings. I have never, for an instant, been sorry to reveal this very personal information. When I experience fleeting thoughts of being too open, I am reminded of a short verse from an unknown author.

> Dare to be a Daniel.
> Dare to stand alone.
> Dare to have a purpose firm.
> Dare to make it known.

The disease of depression isolates its victim and we feel terribly alone. I have encountered many with this disease who relate with great empathy to my journal. On occasion, a reader will come to me, hug me and say, "You wrote this for me, these are my feelings." "I'm not alone." "If you can get well, then I can." Yes !!! They can, and with HELP, TIME and EFFORT most of them do.

I am totally at peace with all of my family, my friends, myself, and my God. My life has been filled with renewed energy, joy, and a deep sense of purpose. If I can help another by writing, speaking, or listening quietly, then I know I have been blest. I firmly believe we receive everything from God, and to help another is our greatest gift to Him.

Thea M. Kellogg

Books

The following is a partial list of books that provided me with guidance, comfort, answers, questions, and opportunities to continue my journey of mental peace and health.

The Holy Bible

The Road Less Traveled
   M. Scott Peck, M.D., Simon and Schuster; ISBN 0-641-24086-2

Jung To Live By
   Eugene Pascal, Ph.L., Warner Books; ISBN 0-446-39294-4

Care of the Soul
   Thomas Moore, HarperPerennial; ISBN 0-06-092224-9

When Bad Things Happen to Good People
   Harold S. Kushner, Avon; ISBN 0-380-60392-6

Around the Year with Emmet Fox
   Emmet Fox, Harper San Francisco; ISBN 0-06-250408-8

The Emmet Fox Treasury (five spirtitual classics)
   Emmet Fox, Harper San Francisco; ISBN 0-06-062860-X

Knowing God
   J.I. Packer, InterVarsity Press; ISBN 0-8308-1650-X

Six Pillars of Self-Esteem
   N. Branden

Overcoming Depression
   Paul A. Hauck, The Westminster Press; ISBN 0-664-24969-8

Overcoming Depression (Revised Edition)
   Demitri Papolos, M.D., and Janice Papolos, HarperPerennial
   ISBN 0-06-096594

Up from Depression
   Leonard Cammer, M.D., Pocket Books, ISBN 0-671-73482-2

You Are Not Alone
   Julia Thorne, HarperPerennial, ISBN 0-06-096977-6

SYMPTOMS OF DEPRESSION

A depressive illness, as defined by the National Institute of Mental Health, is a "whole-body" illness, involving your body, mood, thoughts, and behavior. It affects the way you eat and sleep, the way you feel about yourself, and the way you think about things. A depressive illness is *not* a passing blue mood. It is *not* a sign of personal weakness or a condition that can be willed or wished away. People with depressive illness cannot merely "pull themselves together" and get better. Without treatment, symptoms can last for weeks, months, or years. Appropriate treatment, however can help over 80 percent of those who suffer from depression. Check with your doctor if you need more information.

Not everyone who is depressed experiences every symptom.

- ☐ Persistent sad, anxious, or "empty" mood
- ☐ Feelings of hopelessness, pessimism
- ☐ Feelings of guilt, worthlessness, helplessness
- ☐ Loss of interest or pleasure in hobbies and activities that you once enjoyed, including sex.
- ☐ Insomnia, early-morning awakening, or oversleeping
- ☐ Appetite and/or weight loss or overeating and weight gain
- ☐ Decreased energy, fatigue, being "slowed down"
- ☐ Thoughts of death or suicide, suicide attempts
- ☐ Restlessness, irritability
- ☐ Difficulty concentrating, remembering, making decisions
- ☐ Persistent physical symptoms that do not respond to treatment, such as headaches, digestive disorders, and chronic pain

The National Mental Health Association recommends that if you checked five or more symptoms and they have lasted more than two weeks, tell a doctor.

RESOURCES

HELPING A DEPRESSED PERSON

The most important thing, according to the National Institute of Mental Health, anyone can do for the depressed person is to help him or her get appropriate diagnosis and treatment. This may involve:

- [ ] encouraging the individual to stay with treatment until symptoms begin to abate (several weeks);

- [ ] seeking different treatment if no improvement occurs;

- [ ] making an appointment and accompanying the depressed person to the doctor;

- [ ] possibly monitoring whether the depressed person is taking medication.

The second most important thing is to offer emotional support. This involves:

- [ ] understanding,

- [ ] patience,

- [ ] affection,

- [ ] encouragement.

- [ ] Engage the depressed person in conversation and listen carefully.

- [ ] Do not ignore remarks about suicide. Always report them to the doctor.

- [ ] Invite the depressed person for walks, outings, to the movies, and other activities. Be gently insistent if your invitation is refused.

- [ ] Encourage participation in some activities that once gave pleasure, such as hobbies, sports, religious or cultural activities, but do not push the depressed person to undertake too much too soon. The depressed person needs diversion and company, but too many demands can increase feelings of failure.

Do not accuse the depressed person of faking illness or of laziness, or expect him or her "to snap out of it." Eventually, with treatment, most depressed people do get better. Keep that in mind, and keep reassuring the depressed person that with time and help, he or she will feel better.

RESOURCES

GETTING HELP, LEARNING MORE

There are many caring people available and anxious to help. In addition to help offered by your physician, a number of helping agencies are administered within the U.S. Department of Health & Human Services.

Check your local phone book for a listing in the White Pages under:
  Community Mental Health

Contact the following agencies and support organizations for names of resources in your area:

    National Institute of Mental Health
      DEPRESSION Awareness, Recognition, and Treatment (D/ART)
      Room 10-85, 5600 Fishers Lane
      Rockville, MD 20857
      1-800-421-4211   (for a full range of free educational materials
                         about clinical depression.)

    National Alliance for the Mentally Ill (NAMI)
      NAMI Helpline, 1-800-950-NAMI
      2101 Wilson Boulevard, Suite 302, Arlington, VA 22201
      (703) 524-7600

    National Mental Health Association
      1021 Prince Street, Alexandria, VA 22314
      (703) 684-7722
      1-800-969-NMHA

    National Depressive and Manic-Depressive Association
      730 North Franklin Street, Suite 501
      Chicago, IL 60610
      (312) 642-7243

    American Psychiatric Association
      (202) 682-6220

    American Psychological Association
      (202) 336-5800

About the Author

Thea M. Kellogg lives in an area of Michigan the Native Americans named Leelanau, meaning "The Land of Delight." Leelanau County is located in an area of Michigan that is commonly referred to as the 'little finger of the mitt.' The peninsula is surrounded by the great waters of Lake Michigan and Grand Traverse Bay where the terrain is hilly. Driving along most any road in the County provides spectacular views of one of the most beautiful areas in the world, during any season.

An interest and involvement in writing began for Thea while attending high school and college; but her talents were left dormant for many years. She married Northport native Ray Kellogg in 1964 and raised three sons in an area that is within a mile of her childhood home. In 1992 Thea experienced and triumphed over a serious depression which she has written about in *Visions of Sunsets*.

Thea's work now includes working with people who suffer from depression by offering support and encouragement. She continues to write and is available to speak with public and private groups about depression and her journey to health.

Also by Thea M. Kellogg

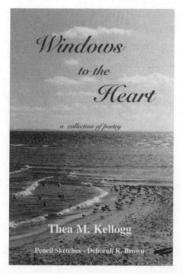

Windows to the Heart
a collection of poetry

Inspired by her Lutheran background, her love of nature, family, and caring friends. This book features spiritual and inspirational poems illustrated with pencil sketches by Northport artist Deborah K. Brown. The cover is a full color photograph taken by Steve Sahs at Gill's Pier, on the Lake Michigan beach between Leland and Northport. As you read you will find God, and you will find nature. $12.00
ISBN 0-9645035-1-4

"Night Bears of Leelanau" poetry poster

A delightful series of poetry posters. 'Bears' was inspired by Thea's husband Ray, to count night bears instead of sheep – because they were more fun and did more! Adults are intrigued by the imagination of the poem, bear enthusiasts love the concept and illustration of bears floating sleepily down along the branches. This 18" x 24" poster also carries a message to children of adventure, promises, sharing, fair play and politeness. $10.00
ISBN 0-9645035-2-2

To order call toll-free 1-800-450-8618

ORDER FORM

Four easy ways to order!

☐   Fax orders: (616) 271-4022

☐   Telephone orders – call toll free: (800) 450-8618
       Have your VISA or MasterCard ready.

☐   Online eMail orders:
       known@traverse.com

☐   Postal orders:
       Known Publishing, P.O. Box 251, Suttons Bay, MI 49682
       Tel: (616) 271-6483

Please send the following:
     I understand that I may return any product for a full refund
     — for any reason, no questions asked.

Qty.	Title	Price	Total
	Visions of Sunsets	12.00	
	Windows to the Heart	12.00	
	Night Bears of Leelanau	10.00	

Michigan residents add 6% Sales Tax

*Shipping:
   Book Rate: $2.00 for first book   Shipping*
     $.75 for each additional book
   Priority Mail: $3.00 per book   Total Enclosed

Payment: __ Check   Credit card: __VISA   __ MasterCard

Card #: _____ Exp. date: __ __ / __ __

Name on card: _____

Signature: _____

Company name _____

Name _____

Address _____

City _____ State _____ Zip _____

Telephone (_____) _____

eMail address: _____

☐ Please send me FREE information about new publications.

─────── **Call toll-free and order now** ───────